Walk in Balance

Other Books by the Authors

The Bear Tribe's Self-Reliance Book
by Sun Bear, Wabun and Nimimosha

Sun Bear: The Path of Power
by Sun Bear, Wabun, and Barry Weinstock

The Medicine Wheel: Earth Astrology
by Sun Bear and Wabun

*Lightseeds: A Compendium of Ancient and Contemporary
Crystal Knowledge* by Wabun Wind and Anderson Reed

Buffalo Hearts by Sun Bear

At Home in the Wilderness by Sun Bear

The People's Lawyers by Marlise James, aka Wabun

WALK IN BALANCE

The Path to Healthy, Happy,
Harmonious Living

SUN BEAR
with Crysalis Mulligan,
Peter Nufer, and Wabun

A FIRESIDE BOOK
Published by Simon & Schuster
New York   London   Toronto   Sydney

FIRESIDE

Rockefeller Center
1230 Avenue of the Americas
New York, New York 10020

FIRESIDE and colophon are registered
trademarks of Simon & Schuster Inc.

Manufactured in the United States of America

20 19 18 17

First Fireside Edition 1992

Library of Congress Cataloging-in-Publication Data
Sun Bear (Chippewa Indian)
    Walk in balance : the path to healthy, happy, harmonious living /
by Sun Bear with Crysalis Mulligan, Peter Nufer, and Wabun. — 1st
Prentice Hall Press ed.
        p. cm.
    Includes bibliographical references.
    1. Health. 2. New Age movement. I. Title.
RA776.5.S85 1989
613—dc20   89-37845
ISBN-13: 978-0-671-76564-4   CIP

Walk in Balance is dedicated to
those people who are trying to heal themselves
and so help with the healing of the earth
and to Wabun
who provides the foundation for so many visions
including mine
—Sun Bear

Acknowledgments

As always, many people have helped me learn the lessons contained in *Walk in Balance*. All those who have been with the Bear Tribe in the past, those who are there now, and all my students and apprentices deserve a lot of credit and thanks. So do all of the health care practitioners—from medical doctors to rolfers to iridologists to suck doctors to psychic surgeons and shamans—who have treated me or talked with me over the years. Special thanks also to those people who have come to me and asked about healing, or about staying well.

Particular thanks, at this time, go to Jaya Houston, Beth Rhiannon, Moon Deer, Michelle Odayinquae, Raven, Shawnodese, Simon Corn Man, Elizabeth Turtle Heart, Robyn Wilson, Singing Pipe Woman, Thunderbird Woman, Mary Fallahy, Joseph LaZenka, Randy North Star, Nimimosha, Gaia, Blue Camas, Matt Ryan, Deborah Shining Star, Yarrow Goding, Casey DuPree, Les Muller, Dennis Price, Betsy Browne, Ken Trogden, Walt Hoesel, Michael and Mickey Shanik, Sunshine Garner, Dr. Barbara Tilmann-Kauf, Tom and Gwenn Oaks, Tom Casey, and everyone else who gives so much of themselves to help the dance continue. Even if you are not mentioned by name, know that you are remembered in my thoughts and prayers.

I want to give real big thanks to Crysalis Mulligan and Peter Sentinel Bear for keeping after me to get the tapes, interviews, and other information that made this book happen. Thanks also to Wabun for all the final work she did on the manuscript. We are all grateful to the Prentice Hall Press folks who have helped produce this book, and the whole Sun Bear series.

Besides humans, many powerful beings from the elemental,

plant, animal, and spirit kingdoms have made this book what it is. I thank them all for their continuing help and support, particularly all the spirits and all the little tobacco-eaters.

And I thank you, dear reader, for being interested in healing yourself and other beings.

—Sun Bear

Crysalis and Sentinel Bear give acknowledgement and thanks to Bat-Sheva, Bim Peistrup, Mark, Jeanne, The Calloways, Linda and Roger Ahearn, The Buckey Women, LP4, Laurel Quinn, Dana, Heather, Julie, and Nancy. Special thanks to Cheron, Maureen Mulligan, Jay, Ricki and Cori, and those Mulligans who have been supportive. Thanks to Michael Kelley who taught the gift of life, the Smith Women, Dancing Wolf, The Los Angeles friends of the Bear Tribe, and especially the Wednesday night pipe group. We gratefully acknowledge Shawnodese, Matt Ryan, Michelle Odayinquae, Singing Pipe Woman, and most of all Sun Bear and Wabun for making this book possible.

Contents

Introduction:
The Vision Continues—
Healing Ourselves,
Healing Our Earth Mother

In *The Bear Tribe's Self-Reliance Book, The Path of Power,* and *The Medicine Wheel,* I told you about visions and my vision. Vision is something that is hoped for but not yet seen. The vision is what leads you on, what directs you and points the way. In the old times, each young man was encouraged to seek a vision, and native women were also free to do this. In seeking the vision, one would go out and pray. "What shall be my purpose in life, Great Spirit? How can I best serve the needs of my people? What is my part in the universe?" With the vision comes the power of direction.

In several of my visions, I saw a time when we would all live together as brothers and sisters, Indian and non-Indian alike. I saw the Earth Mother being healed as people began to show a love for the land. But first, I saw the possibility of a time of great desolation, a time of hunger, drought, and illness. From my visions I knew I must teach people to be self-reliant, to heal themselves and this planet, our Earth Mother.

As time went on, I began my work with The Bear Tribe Medicine Society. Later, the vision of the Medicine Wheel came to me and then started to unfold.

In my vision of the Medicine Wheel, I saw an inner and outer circle of stones with rocks placed like the spokes of a wheel connecting the two. Inside the sacred circle was the buffalo skull. People wearing animal costumes and headdresses represented the four directions and all the other powers of the universe.

Each person was singing the song of his season, of his mineral, of his plant, and of his totem animal. And they were singing songs for the healing of the Earth Mother.

A leader among them was saying, "Let the medicine of the sacred circle prevail. Let many people across the land come to the circle and make prayers for the healing of the Earth Mother. Let the circles of the Medicine Wheel come back." They have. Since 1980 the Bear Tribe has sponsored an average of four Medicine Wheel Gatherings each year. Usually 400 to 1,200 people attend each gathering, and many of them go on to build their own Medicine Wheels.

In the years since my first vision much work has been done to increase harmony between people and the Earth Mother. I am very happy to continue to live by my visions and see them grow. It is good to see people becoming more self-reliant and utilizing many of the tools we have made available.

Now I see a need for a better understanding of health and healing on a personal level. Learning to be self-reliant in healing yourself is of utmost importance. The stronger and healthier we are as spiritual warriors, the more we will have to give of ourselves to the continual healing of the Earth Mother. Good health makes it easier for us to do our part in the universe, to serve our people, and for each of us to fulfill our personal life visions.

To have a lifetime plan of action to support and promote your spiritual, physical, emotional, and mental well-being is a wise path to walk. In this book we will be sharing many specific tools that will assist you to walk in balance and to achieve the best health possible.

Walk in Balance first gives you a philosophy that encourages health. Ninety percent of all illness begins in the head. You must get rid of the mind creatures which predispose you to illness. Then, by learning what is good for you, opening up to the universe, and finding ways to be happier, you can begin working toward a longer and more fulfilling life.

For your work to be successful you need the proper tools— acceptance of the life force in *all* its forms, good diet, and revitalizing exercise. *Walk in Balance* discusses all these tools, and helps you to plan your own healthful path to power.

Given the amount of negative attitudes we've all been fed from birth, and the state of the environment, many of us will experience some form of dis-ease. The final chapters of *Walk in Balance* are about different ways of preventing dis-ease and of dealing with illness if it happens—herbal remedies, healing ceremonies, other natural alternatives, resources, and people. This book is a comprehensive manual to help you walk in balance, health, and beauty on the Earth Mother.

Two new coauthors have joined Wabun and me in preparing *Walk in Balance*. They are Crysalis Mulligan and Peter Sentinel Bear Nufer.

Crysalis Mulligan (Emerging Butterfly Woman) is one of my apprentices, a pipe woman, founder of the Nurture Nature Program, and an avid environmentalist and conservationist. Crysalis is a holistic healer who has been working with stone therapy for almost a decade. She owns crystal mining claims and has been mining, researching, and sharing her crystal knowledge for the same amount of time.

In her early twenties, she developed health problems. With diet, nutrition, a spiritual path, the support of traditional and holistic medicine, and a good attitude she has added years to her life. She feels that it is not everyone's path to experience total healing. For many "walking in balance" means being alive and fulfilled despite some forms of dis-ease. She brings her first-hand experience dealing with illness and healing to the writing of this book.

Peter Sentinel Bear Nufer is an acclaimed survivalist and camping expert. As a wilderness experience trainer and educator, Sentinel Bear has brought a unique hands-on perspective of the wilds to many people.

Peter is accredited within the television industry as an associate producer, assistant director, and director of photography on three documentaries that were Emmy-nominated and given bronze medals by the Film and Television Festival of New York.

He is a pipecarrier who works in affiliation with Sun Bear and The Bear Tribe. Crysalis and Peter Sentinel Bear Nufer are co-owners of the Red Road Trading Company.

The illness and death of his father caused Peter to explore alternative methods of health and healing. Over the years, Peter has found diet, exercise, and, most of all, attitude to be the best formula for continued health and happiness.

Over the years, Wabun and I have also worked with a variety of preventive medicine techniques—and with illness when it has occurred. We've experienced self-healing, ceremonial healing, and a good number of the alternative methods we write about. Among the four of us, we've also experienced enough of western medicine to know some ways to make it work better for you.

Life goes a lot smoother when you have your health, and we hope this book will help you in that regard. We also hope it will help you recognize it is possible to walk in balance even during times of dis-ease.

—Sun Bear

1 | The Mind Creatures

Ninety percent of all illness begins in our heads. Ingrained negative thought patterns, many of them left over from our childhoods, help create illness if we hold on to them. I even know native medicine men whose illnesses resulted from internalized anger patterns for which they had no release. Two of these medicine men died of cancer. One let the anger eat away at him until he got stomach cancer. The other kept it in his head until he got brain cancer. Sadness, fear, depression, or plain grouchiness can do the same thing. By the time an illness has become a firm physical reality, tracing and reversing the original negative energy patterns may be quite challenging, and very time consuming. It could even take more time than a person may have left.

Consequently, prevention is an important thing for you to understand. You can experience life as a beautiful dance if you learn to become a spiritual warrior—a person capable of defending your own destiny. Defending your destiny is your given right and your responsibility. In order to be a spiritual warrior you must begin by cleaning up your own act, ridding yourself of the things that cause you pain and frustration. You need either to digest or disgorge the things that are eating at you, no matter how long they've been doing so. Preventive care on all levels of being is mandatory to well-being.

There is truth to the adage, "It is not what you eat but what eats you." It is the deep-down gut-level things that make you feel unhappy, that give you a sense of anger, turmoil, sadness, helplessness, or frustration in your life that eventually can give you problems. These emotions literally take power over you. I call these patterns mind creatures because they actually like to get inside your head and eat at you.

Don't despair! Everybody has mind creatures and there are viable tools to help free you from these negative chains of thought and emotion. It is your choice whether or not to utilize these tools. Only you can take charge of your life and integrate new information and habits that can break these chains. This can be a painful process, but, with perseverance, joy can follow.

The first step is to recognize your patterns of thought and feeling. If thinking of your ex-husband, ex-wife, boyfriend, girlfriend, mother, father, or coworker makes you "hot" with anger, lust, or another strong emotion, you may be experiencing a negative emotional bond that could become a mind creature. Job-related worries, concerns over debt, a negative situation you've experienced, or an unresolved traumatic childhood experience can also cause such bonds. Frequently we don't even realize we are bothered by something. I periodically take time to explore myself emotionally to see if I am holding on to any negativities. If you don't take time to check, these negative charges become buried in you. They burrow into your emotions encouraging internal dissension. They canal through your being in search of a discharge. On a spiritual plane, they sabotage your attempts to reinstate inner harmony. Such frustrations and pressures compound, increasing anxiety, resulting in physical tensions that create a virtual paradise for illness. Eventually dis-ease and physical illness may begin to surface.

Imagine your stress level is like a long horizontal board nailed firmly to a sturdy crate at each end. This structure is basically strong and durable. However, if you place heavier and heavier weights on the center of the board eventually it will bend and then break under the pressure. Your *resistance* to stress and disease is like this board. You must carefully determine the amount of pressure and stress you can take before you bend too far and break down physically or emotionally. To do this it is necessary to realize how much the pressures in your life put you at risk.

In the old days my people did not experience many of the stresses that are a part of contemporary life. Modern people recognize this on some level. A lot of you work hard your whole lives so you can retire to a house or a camper in the middle of the woods and spend your time fishing, gardening, taking care of the basics, and living a lot like the native people of old.

People who want to "live like the Indians" have a good idea of what it takes to reduce stress. Living close to nature, taking time to see the trees and hear the birds, and taking care of life's essentials are all great stressbusting methods. I'll tell you more about them in later chapters.

Saying that you can control your stress level and mind creatures is not saying that you control your destiny completely. Only the Great Spirit who is within and around all of life sees the whole of our universe. The whys and whats of our destiny are not even the central issues here. I want to emphasize that you should do the best you can with the control you have over your life and health. Clean up your past and lay a foundation for your future, so that you may live the most rewarding life possible in your present.

DO YOU CREATE YOUR OWN REALITY?

Today it is very popular to encourage people to believe they are totally responsible for absolutely everything that happens to them in their lives. Some people say you can create perfection and miracles through the power of thought alone. Creative manifestation is well and good for basically healthy people who can have a good job, a nice home and car, manageable debt, and a youthful or strong constitution.

However, "You create your own reality" can be a cruel philosophy to someone starving in a third world country, a victim of violent abuse, a person who is fighting for his life or sanity, or one who is unemployable and homeless. Yes, we do create our realities but in complex and long-term ways. For someone in a bad situation, solving the crisis at hand must take priority over philosophical processing. This popular belief that we can create perfection and miracles is sound when applied to groups of people who are in a position to become accountable human beings, as long as it isn't used as a guilt-inducing device. However, a mother with starving children needs food not philosophy.

Being a spiritual warrior is knowing the tools available to you and knowing which ones are most appropriate in any given circumstance. Consider a situation in which a father is dying from a chronic disease. His children feel they are being abandoned, and they fear being sentenced to the same death through heredity. His spouse, consumed with the loss, must also be concerned with survival and with extensive medical bills. And the man is losing his very breath of life.

Do you think that telling him "Well, you created this," is going to make him feel better? No. In these circumstances, this philosophy brings no relief or understanding. This man must experience the process of death and dying. As explained by my friend Dr. Elizabeth Kubler-Ross in her book *Death and Dying*, that process is denial, isolation, anger, bargaining, depression, acceptance, and then hope. After accepting his own death, this man needs to make peace with his family, and review their survival abilities. After all that, he needs a philosophy that will provide him with hope, not guilt.

Consider a situation in which parents have a child with cancer. They have chosen to treat the child through the natural therapies they feel will result in the most improvement and the least pain. Their former doctor takes them to court accusing them of neglecting their child's health. They are then forced to subject the child to a painful therapy in which they have no belief. Will they benefit by considering if, how, and why they created this reality, or will such contemplation take all the fight out of them?

Once a reporter for a New Age magazine asked me if I was familiar with the "You create your own reality" philosophy. When I said I was, he asked if I had any idea why the Indians created the reality of living in poverty on reservations. Ignoring his unbelievable lack of familiarity with history, I answered, " 'You create your own reality,' like any philosophy, contains a lot of bullchips." (Anyway, the word I used sounded like bullchips.)

My belief is "If a philosophy doesn't grow corn, I don't want to hear about it." It takes fertilizer to grow corn. Sometimes I think certain new philosophies are too rich in one of the best natural fertilizers, and too lacking in grounding and compassion.

THE PATH OF THE SPIRITUAL WARRIOR
When choosing your spiritual warrior path, your first consideration must be to find a plan that works for your needs and life patterns. Through this process of choice, a plan can be conceived

4

or "created" by you that will benefit the way you live the rest of your life. It is the process of choice and individualization that will enable your plan to be successful. Since many tools are available, it is okay to try different methods until you find the health-building tools appropriate for you. If you are in a crisis situation, deal first with the crisis and then build your foundation. Don't cook your dinner over the fire that is burning down your house.

If one of your tools is making you feel guilty, get rid of it. Guilt is the most wasteful emotion we experience. It won't always be fun to get well, but to stay well you need to see the fun side of life. Don't hide from your issues, but don't beat yourself up emotionally in order to clear out negative patterns. Clearing negative energy can be painful, but need not be ruthless.

It comes down to how you deal or don't deal with your own energy field. Get rid of the garbage that keeps you from creating the energy field that is truly you, the life force you are meant to be. Remember, you are part of the Creator, just like the plants and the birds.

GETTING RID OF YOUR GARBAGE

We are the bottom line. If we want, we can learn how to build a circle of energy and power that is unbeatable. But first, we have to get rid of our own garbage. The native elders had many ways to do this.

The Mayan people of Mexico would stand in a stream of flowing water. They would talk out over the water all that concerned them: their angers, fears, sorrows, or troubles. Water is a moving life energy. It would take all the emotions they poured out of themselves into the current and away from them.

The native people up in northern California also have a way to rid themselves of negativity. They have what they call the Bear Dance. A man in a bear costume dances around a circle of people. As he dances, the people use wormwood switches to whack him while simultaneously speaking about the things in their lives that have been bothering them. They speak all their anger, all their negativities out at this bear. When they are emotionally depleted the bear goes down into the stream. There he washes the anger and negativity off and they flow away down stream.

Some native people of the Southwest have another dance.

Dressed in yellow and black outfits and armed with swords, they dance through the village, singing, chanting, and rattling, driving out the negative forces as they go. Behind them come people with brooms that are usually made out of cedar bough. They sweep away anything that is left over. Then the corn maiden comes and sprinkles a blessing of cornmeal throughout the village. Cornmeal is a sacred blessing.

Most native people around the world had some way of letting people get rid of negativity. The ancient Hebrews used a goat in much the same way northern Californians used a bear. From their practice comes the term "scapegoat." During some fiestas, Mexican people would make a papier-mâché figure they called "Dr. Gloom." They would put their negative thoughts and feelings on pieces of paper which they would stuff into the figure. Then they would burn him and watch their mind creatures go up in smoke.

I teach people an exercise called "Dig a hole," and I will give you complete instructions for that in the chapter on ceremonial healing.

Whether you choose a native method of getting rid of negativity or a more contemporary one is not as important as choosing one and sticking with it. There are many powerful modern methods that can be very successful for releasing negative patterns, very old deep hurts, frustrations, compulsions, and habits inbred in people since birth. The cathartic therapies such as orgonomy, Gestalt, bioenergetics, radix, rebirth, primal scream, and holotropic work are particularly good in this regard. These therapies combine counseling with body and breath work. If you exhibit compulsive behavior or have been exposed to compulsions through family members, there are a large variety of "twelve-step programs" such as Alcoholics Anonymous, Al-Anon, Adult Children of Alcoholics, Sex-Aholics, Debtors-Anonymous, and Overeaters Anonymous, which can help. They are listed in your phone book and are free.

For some people high-impact, compact workshops that encourage personal accountability can be phenomenal catalysts that result in major breakthroughs in a relatively short period of time. My ten-day screening program is one such workshop. Vision Quest programs are another. It's good to have a support group or back-up therapy program to help process the incredible transformation that can take place. The Bear Tribe has such support groups in many regions of the country.

Expressing yourself through creative outlets is another way to get in touch with the positive aspects of your inner self. Beading, pottery, leatherworking, and other crafts were traditional native ways of relaxing, releasing, and praying. For every bead strung, for every turn of the potter's wheel, for every pull of sinew through leather the craftsperson said a prayer. You can still do this today and apply it to painting, doing needlepoint, acting, singing, dancing, exercising, or any other art that expresses the true you.

To release old negative patterns and build new positive ones, you should strive for a balance of spirituality, creativity, work, enjoyment, exercise, diet, and self-examination.

There are no guarantees in life. However, avoiding emotional, physical, mental and spiritual stagnation, and or stress will certainly give you an edge in your favor. There is an old quote that says "For evil to happen, all that is necessary is for good men to do nothing." Remember, if you want action in your life you must take it.

2 | Learning What's Good for You

Nothing is more critical in life than discovering what is good for you. By understanding and fulfilling your unique needs, and applying your own visions, dreams, and principles to your life you can find your proper path and keep most mind creatures away. Many of us have been raised to believe that the values and principles handed down generationally are enough. In some cases they are, but in our fast-changing world many of us need a larger variety of goals than our parents did to live full, happy, and responsible lives. *Only you can determine what will make your life truly work for you.*

Having a vision or philosophy that is uniquely yours and works for you is a great tool. This philosophy must work on an everyday basis. If it's so esoteric that you can't manage to go to work or complete your responsibilities on a physical plane, then you'd better look for a more realistic approach to life and spirit. My philosophy, "If it doesn't grow corn I don't want to hear about it," is not meant only in a spiritual sense, but in a practical earth sense. We are earth beings. Our daily lives and spiritual lives need to work together so we have whatever we need, from food to health to love and fulfilling work.

We earth beings constantly need to find ways to nourish ourselves on physical, mental, emotional, and spiritual planes. When we feel nourished we are much more able to nurture others and the earth. Spirit—the Creator—wants to help us. The more in tune we are with Spirit, the wider the doors through which help can come. The clearer we call to Spirit, the clearer will be our answer. The more aware we become of how truly we are guided and helped by Spirit, or how "conscious" we are, the more Spirit will respond.

For this help, we should remember to give thanks often and honor the forces that support us.

Finding your spirit path should be a real part of your physical life on this earth. Spirit is not something you wait to experience in Heaven. Spirit can and is realized on this plane. In Mexico I've seen the people doing ceremonies in their corn fields, their homes, even in their gardens. Everywhere in their lives they acknowledge the forces and powers. These people are not wealthy, yet they live good lives. They live naturally, close to the earth. They have a balance they respect and honor.

On Vision Mountain everywhere you look you see signs of the way we honor the Spiritkeepers. There are prayer feathers hanging in our shelters, our barns, and our vehicles. As you walk the land you may come across the Medicine Wheel that honors the balance of all of life and teaches us about ourselves on a daily basis.

Our sweatlodge is near a spring and a grove of trees. Higher up you will come across the Earth Mound where prayers and offerings are made in honor of our Earth Mother, or the Air Mound, or the Sacred Spring. There are other sacred areas to honor the moon and other powerful elements of life. Before each meal we come together in a circle, join hearts and hands and make a prayer of thanks to Great Spirit and to all the kingdoms that gave of themselves so our lives might continue. Each week we have a sacred pipe ceremony so we may come together in prayer. These are some of the many ways we acknowledge Spirit. Because we make this effort, Spirit responds and helps guide our lives.

It is very important to utilize what you have available to you in your life and to be thankful for it. Take care of the realities of having a full belly and clothes on your back, and then be open to the fun, games, and beauty life offers. I feel we are here for a much higher purpose than to just go back and forth to work every day, pounding on typewriters and watching TV. Finding that greater consciousness, that philosophy or vision that will help you reach out, play, work, and love with spirituality is what life is all about.

I once had a powerful dream in which I was standing under a tall tree by a large cage made from wood saplings. There were five people in the cage. I was on one side of the cage and a big grizzly bear was on the other. We were shaking this cage back and forth between us. When I woke up I thought about it for a minute. I realized this is what I am doing in life. With the help of the Bear Spirit I am rattling people's cages. I am doing the work Spirit has guided me to do and am enjoying life along the way. This is my path. What is yours?

KICK UP YOUR HEELS

I have come to the conclusion there are no guilties and no innocents in the world. Bad and good will happen, and our responsibility is to do the best we can as honestly as we can. To do your best, it is your responsibility to explore and then implement what is truly good for you. This means assessing whether the values instilled in you during your formative years are still truly functional, beneficial to your life and supportive of yourself, our planet, and society in a healthy, responsible manner. This assessment is part of the sacred dance and will help you to find out what your path really is. Many people live out their lives as replicas of their parents; they never question how or if they were programmed. In some cases this works out fine; in others, it doesn't. But accepting someone else's vision or values makes you a one-legged dancer. If you are a carbon copy of your parents or anybody else you might never learn your own dance. Find out just whose legs you're dancing on, then get out there and kick up both heels.

After exploring yourself and your values you may say, "Hey, this is good," and not feel a need to change or grow. However, you may say, "This is not working for me, I need change and growth." If this is the case, then follow your heart and spirit. Be brave. Find out what your true path is. Listen to your intuition. Walk a new path. If it feels good then walk some more. If it doesn't seem quite right check out another avenue. But don't stop searching. The hunt isn't over until both your heart and belly are full. In this age of awareness so many dances are available. Look around, see what's happening in your community. If something draws your interest, don't stagnate or be indecisive or afraid. Go for it. It's like buying a new pair of shoes. Try a few pairs on, but don't buy any until you find a pair that really fits.

Whether you are willing to find your own legs and wholeheartedly kick up your heels can affect your health. Many people stay sick because of their old prejudices and conditioning. This is one of the greatest tragedies of this society. People will say, "Oh, I couldn't try a homeopathic remedy because the doctor wouldn't want me to," or "I couldn't be healed by this person because that would be contrary to my religious beliefs." Or, "Does he have credentials, does he have a degree to prove he knows how to heal me?"

A lot of people are wheeled into cemeteries every day because of their prejudices. Be sure you don't allow prejudices to keep you from healing yourself.

WHAT FOODS ARE GOOD FOR YOU?

Often food prejudices keep people from trying new types of diets that could help. A lot of people in this country grew up on a strictly meat and potatoes diet. They believed this was good nutrition. Now that we have the largest obesity problem in the world and a generation of adults dying from heart disease, hypertension, and cancer we are finding out that this diet high in fatty meat and processed foods is not very nutritional. Now even the mainstream cereal companies are pushing "all natural high fiber cereals" and fast food chain restaurants are adding "light" foods to their menus. Not only is a largely fast food diet like eating cancer and gallbladder bombs, but the styrofoam packaging destroys our fragile ozone layer. When you indulge at fast food joints you are hurting not only your body but also the body of the planet. Public outcry about these environmental issues has made a difference in the practices of some chains. If you do sometimes eat fast food, patronize those places that demonstrate nutritional and environmental consciousness.

Watch what you buy at the supermarket. The ready-made processed foods loaded with sugar and salt are not about nutrition. They are about corporate profit. Look at economic reports and judge for yourself the amount of money being made at the expense of the planet and peoples' health. Check books that rate food corporations according to their planetary concern, and only buy from those that score highly.

Recently I had some young men from the city come out to visit me on wood-cutting day and help with the labor. After about an hour-and-a-half they were ready to drop from exhaustion. They said, "Sun Bear, can't we take a break?" Now these guys were only about twenty years old. I looked at them, smiled, and said, "Oh, I know you. You are the Post Toasties generation. You are the people who have grown up on fast foods and don't have any stamina left."

Human conditioning is more dangerous than all the atomic bombs in the world. Conditioning has resulted in the atomic threat. We've been conditioned to think we're all going to heaven so we don't have to take responsibility for the Earth Mother, or for our bodies. Most people don't think beyond their responsibility for their own home and family. As a result we have polluted the planet. This conditioning is why we have been able to justify destroying the South American rain forests, exploit much of the Third World, torch Vietnam, and annihilate Hiroshima.

THE WAITING GAME

I know people who have a lot of excuses. They blame their lives on exterior things. Frequently I hear "waiting" stories from people who are waiting for life to happen. They are waiting to get married or waiting for the right job. Then there's the big wait, waiting for their kids to grow up. Then they wait for retirement. All they have left after that is to wait for the cemetary. They have never lived or experienced their own lives. They have locked themselves into a little box because of conditioning that has been put on them by other people.

If you let other people run your life and take power over you, you are setting yourself up for a miserable existence. Figure out what, if anything, is bothering you and deal with it. If it is the government, make a stand, vote differently, write your congressmen, senators, or the president. Tell them how you feel. If you suffer from negative conditioning from your parents, the church, an old lover, etc., then you need to do emotional release work to free yourself from these bonds. This will take time and courage, but it is worth it. Your only other option is to be a slave to other people's quirks, hangups, ideals, dreams, and principles. That option makes you a zombie drifting in the wake of the living.

Every human being has a right and responsibility to fulfill her destiny. To exercise them, you must stay in control of your own personal being. When you witness, expose, or are subjected to injustices, it is your responsibility to do what you can to right the wrong. You may not be able to change the source of injustice but you can break the pattern and stop the momentum.

If you don't do anything about injustice it will affect you not only emotionally, but also physically. Deep inside you a voice begins to grind, saying "Hey, I must be sick to give up on myself, my dreams, and my reality. I'm no good and I deserve to be sick." Ailments result and you begin to feed this negative energy.

There have been times when I have counseled others about illness and at some point I've thought "Nobody is coming up with answers. Everybody is just spouting off and telling goofy stories." So I would go and pray and say "Hey Creator what is this about?" One time the Creator told me that sicknesses are the wolves that thin the human herd. They are like the wolf that circles around a herd of animals, observing which one is tired or frail, then going in for the kill. This is how sickness works.

Sickness works on people who have allowed themselves to get low energy or to be off balance, be it in their diet or how they relate to life. Sometimes they relate to life with too little energy or enthusiasm, almost like they've resigned from the human race. Other times they relate with so much energy and so few checks they allow themselves to get burned out. Sickness lurks like a hunting animal, then grabs a person and has them for lunch. Maintaining balance and harmony is the only way to prevent this from happening.

I've had certain illnesses so I understand this on a personal basis. The spirits kicked me in the rear and said, "Hey, you know you've got a good head, but you have to have a body to carry it around on the physical plane. Because this is a physical planet. No physical body, no life. Those are the facts."

Now, I am near sixty and I feel like I'm thirty-five. I took back my power over my body and stopped allowing myself to do the things that put me in a weakened state. I am on the road teaching and lecturing 90 percent of the year. Sometimes I start to get run down and I stop myself. I'll be careful to balance my diet, exercise, do a sweatlodge, or accept massage and other forms of healing that keep me balanced and strong. Now I don't just say, "Okay I'm going to heal myself." I back up self-healing with tools I have on the physical plane, like the ones I've mentioned. I am clear about what my path is and about the tools that get me back on my path if I start to detour. And I have learned to let others help me, which is the primary tool against burn-out.

BUY YOUR OWN TICKET

What is your path? This is the big question. The Kahuna people say that at this time all of humanity is here for a purpose. I believe this very strongly. Whether you find and fulfill that purpose is up to each one of you. There is no requirement to do so. There is no big broadcast from the heavens saying you must be enlightened. It is not set up this way.

You have to reach out in order to know for yourself what your path and purpose in life is. That is what it is about. When you say "I want to know something else beyond mere existence," is when Spirit will open up the universe and start working with you.

You must tap into your intuitive energy in order to find your way to the next level of consciousness and power. This will be challenging because in today's society you are taught to think and not feel. You want to think everything. But it is intuition that will guide you to a new and powerful way. This will be your way and your path. Call to Spirit and ask for direction. Open up intuitively so that you can hear the answers that Spirit has for you. Ceremony, meditation, prayer, quiet, and solitude can help you develop this. These are good tools that can help you find the path of the undying warrior.

A wonderful thing is happening in our time. A nation of people from countries, races, and tribes all over the world are reaching for and coming to the same level of consciousness. You may well be on the path to joining up with this nation of people. Welcome.

Life can be like a wonderful carnival ride. The only way you won't get to go for the ride is if you don't get your own ticket. So explore what tickets are available and come aboard. There is a joke about the man who prayed every day to win the lottery and never did. Finally, one day he got down on his knees and said, "Lord, Lord, why do you ignore my prayers? Please Lord, oh please, hear me and answer my prayers to win the lottery!" Suddenly, a loud voice from heaven says, "Meet me half way—buy a ticket!" Like this man, you must do your part to make life happen for you.

Embrace each moment. Caress each day with a love for life and life will love and caress you.

Sacred knowledge is available to us if we learn what is good for us, open up, and make ourselves available to it. Much of learning what is good for you is simply to listen, so that when help or assistance is available you are open to receiving it.

Once I was spending an afternoon in a mountain area. I wanted to walk further up this mountain. I almost did, but I realized I was being given a message not to go any further. Rather than ignore the message, I quieted myself and listened. It was Spirit telling me not to go up the mountain but to stay where I was. So I lay down and started praying. I was in a state of being half-asleep and half-awake when I heard singing, children playing, and cannon fire. I looked around but there was no one there, only the stones and rocks that had been there for eons. I closed my eyes and went deeper into sleep. Then the dreams began. These dreams told me a long and lovely story.

After a period, I awoke feeling like Rip Van Winkle. I remembered vast amounts of knowledge and knew it was the history of events about this area. When I met up with the people I was traveling with, I shared the knowledge I had received. They were familiar with the area and confirmed that the information I had learned was true. The spirits of the stones had bestowed on me a special tour through history. Because I was willing to slow down, stop, listen, and receive I gained much valuable knowledge about a very special place and time. Since this experience I find that I have dreams like this one in many areas.

3 | Happiness Is the Best Medicine

The most important ingredient for good health is happiness. Happiness is the greatest medicine. I am happy 95 percent of the time. The reason I am capable of this much happiness is because I am doing things I believe in. I like my work. I have good and loving people around me. In short, I am living my life as I want to.

I'm constantly thankful I have two legs and two arms that help me get around. I have a brain that gives me the opportunity to learn, to make my own decisions, and to expand. I have a heart that pumps the life force through me, and I have reasonably good health. I am fortunate! I have followed my own advice and created an interesting life, doing things I like and making a living at them. How can I be anything but happy?

When a person is not happy with his life, he should make it a priority to correct this situation. It may not happen instantaneously, but, however long it takes and no matter how difficult the changes may be, he'll find no more important quest in his lifetime. Much of your ability to experience happiness is the result of a sense of worth or well-being about yourself, even in challenging and difficult situations.

You can help to create your happiness by expanding on what makes you feel good, continually feeling it, feeding it, nurturing it, and increasing it. At the same time, continue to move away from the things that cause discontent and make you unhappy.

It takes courage to love yourself and your world. So again, it comes back to doing work and having attitudes that will allow you to know you are a good individual, a sacred human being.

Something I do every day is wake up and thank the Great Spirit I am alive. Everyday I reach out to create and maintain an energy field of thankfulness and happiness. By conscious actions I sustain myself in a happy state 95 percent of the time. Negative people can't penetrate my happiness. People come up to me and say, "I can't stand you Sun Bear. You're too positive." After saying that, these kind of people flee from me, and I'm not exposed to their negativity.

I take care of shelter, food, happiness, and clothes and consider all else a bonus. And I remember everything can be a source of humor, even clothing and the way you wear it. For instance, basically I have no hips. This means my shirt tail is always hanging out and my pants tend to fall down. But I have learned to work with what life and nature give me. People used to take bets on whether or not I was going to lose my pants during certain lectures. I have a photo of a group of my male students all lined up doing an imitation of me. It is a shot of them from the back, and all their pants are down enough so that their vertical smiles show. Humor is very important. I run in the other direction from anyone who claims to be spiritual and doesn't have a sense of humor.

It has been said that the most dangerous people in the world are the extreme moralists, such as Hitler and the Ayatollah Khomeini. They are not humorous or caring men. Their philosophy basically was, and is, "I am right or you are dead." For one reason or another, some people seem to go to extremes. They miss the point that so much of life is creating a balance and maintaining a good outlook, that so much of life is attitude.

I let problems wash over me like water over a duck's back. I listen to people, and I help when I can but I don't take their problems on and let them weigh me down. I try to do the same with problems that arise in my own life. After all, worrying rarely solves anything.

I make it a point not to waste my energy trying to change people who don't want to change. If someone wants to spend their time moaning about life, I can't change that. But I can get out of their way!

I don't let family—extended or blood—or other loved ones rob me of energy. People can trip me up sometimes and I have to make some hard decisions. Somebody I love very much may get into a cycle of energy where they are wanting to take too many nibbles out of me. This causes me to lose my balance. If this happens I have to say "Hey, you know I really love you but I can't stand that treatment." Finally I might have to say "Bless you, but I don't need that." Some of you may need to look at how you walk your sacred path. You may be allowing someone to take little nibbles out of you. Are you possibly a nibbler yourself? It isn't good either to nibble or to be nibbled. It doesn't help anyone or change anything. In fact, nibbling often keeps people from changing.

THE MAGIC MIRROR

I know a famous authoress who now is living a very good and happy life. She hasn't always been either famous or happy. She used to be a dull, drab, bored, and unhappy housewife who wanted to write. But she was afraid she might be successful if she started writing. Though it may sound strange, many people are afraid of success because of the changes it can bring in their lives. This woman was so afraid of success that she would not do the things that might make her happy.

She came to one of my workshops and heard me talk about how I stand in front of the mirror in the morning after I make my prayers. I look at myself, first make some faces so that I don't take it all too seriously, and then I tell myself I'm a good, handsome, and deserving person. I greet myself and give myself encouragements for the day. When I leave the mirror I am ready to face life with a smile.

This woman tried the mirror exercise first to convince herself she deserved to be happy, then to convince herself she deserved success. The exercise seemed to work for her.

One of these days I'm going to produce my "Magic Mirror." This will be for people just beginning to realize they deserve happiness. The mirror will tell them all the good things they need to hear about themselves until they can do this on their own.

LAUGH MEDICINE

Before I leave my mirror in the morning, sometimes I take a minute to look at myself and laugh. Besides putting life in perspective, it encourages my laugh medicine for that day. And I believe laughter is an important medicine.

Laughter is more than just an expression of mirth. Norman Cousins, an adjunct professor of medical humanities at the UCLA School of Medicine, in *Anatomy of an Illness* says laughter is like

18

inner jogging. It causes the muscles to contract, particularly those of the abdomen, chest and shoulders. It also increases heart rate, respiration rate, and blood pressure so that muscles are more relaxed after laughter, and heart rate and blood pressure swing below normal the way they do after jogging or other exercise.

I always enjoy telling people about how Norman Cousins became involved in teaching about laughter and its auspicious effects. As he describes it in his book, Mr. Cousins became quite ill and was hospitalized. The prognosis wasn't good. He didn't buy the bad news the doctors were giving him. He decided he'd stand a better chance of healing outside of the hospital, so he got a hotel room and had friends bring him in all the funny movies and things they could. He figured he might as well try to enjoy himself. As time went on and he laughed more and more, he began to feel better and he began to get better.

After his recovery, he decided to spend time taking the message of the benefit of laughter to the medical profession and to the general public. As the result of his writings and work about this, some hospitals now have laughter rooms and there are a number of people going around the country lecturing about the benefits of laughter.

Laughter can also help reduce pain in some cases. Dr. William Fry of Stanford University has found there is an increase in respiratory activity, muscular activity, heart rate and oxygen exchange during laughter. The stimulation to the cardiovascular system, nervous system, and pituitary gland caused by laughing, indirectly stimulates the production of endorphins, the body's natural pain-reducing enzymes.

The Laughter Project at the University of California at Santa Barbara has found laughter does as well at reducing stress as more complex biofeedback training programs. By reducing stress and lowering blood pressure, laughter decreases the chance of heart attack and stroke.

TWO GRANDMOTHERS
Sentinel Bear tells the story of his two grandmothers. One was a down-to-earth woman who enjoyed every second of living. She was curious, had a good relationship with her Creator and never worried too much about anything. She survived a kidney operation

at the age of eighty-eight and a leg amputation at the age of ninety-three.

She became the town crier of her convalescence home and stayed busy crocheting lap robes for the other patients at her hospital and for the veterans at the Veterans Hospital in Los Angeles. She always had an open ear for other people's problems and was forever saying prayers for someone. Once you were on her list for rosaries you were on it forever. All you had to do to get on her list was ask.

She could be cantankerous one minute, innocent the next, then flash you a mischievous twinkle that told you it was all a joke anyway. Life was fun for her and although she often said, in her later years, that she was tired and just wanted the Lord to take her, there was one thing she really wanted to do before she died. She wanted to have one last party at which she was the guest of honor. One month after celebrating her 100th birthday she passed on in her sleep.

She stayed sharp right up to the end, and Sentinel Bear believes that she did so because she stayed interested in life and the things happening around her. She met life on her own terms and treated each challenge as an opportunity. She had a subtle, yet extraordinary understanding of her life, and she knew it.

In contrast, his other grandmother was afraid of life, suspicious of those around her, and worried about almost everything. She had no apparent relationship with her Creator. Though she was a good woman and loved her family, she was more self-centered than his other grandmother. She was never involved with anything that did not immediately affect her. She let her fears control her life. She spent her final years in senility, wanting nothing to do with the people around her. She was withdrawn and remote. Her death at the age of sixty-seven seemed more a shrinking away from life than a transition to another form of being.

Sentinel Bear remembers the two women braiding his sister's pigtails, one on each tail. The tail braided by his cheerful grandmother was tight, solid, and would last forever. The tail braided by his anxious grandmother was loose, frail, and fell out within the hour. Those pigtails provided an accurate image of each woman's attitude toward life.

A cheerful attitude is a recurring theme in many older people's lives. This attitude, in fact, is one of the reasons they live so long. Although Sentinel Bear's cheerful grandmother had a troublesome heart, lost a kidney, and had a leg amputated, she still saw the joy in life. After she lost her leg, a physical therapist made several fruitless attempts at teaching her to use a walker. She said, "Why in hell do I want to learn to use that thing when, after ninty-three years, I finally have a chance to sit down."

Not only did this woman maintain a certain amount of control over her life, but also she always saw the positive side of any situation. Being in a wheelchair never slowed her down a bit. Her happy attitude was the foundation for her long and fulfilling life and her laughter was its capstone.

A GOOD ATTITUDE CAN KEEP YOU GOING

So much of life is attitude! Even if your health is suffering, try to enjoy life in the ways you can. I know people in wheelchairs and with other special abilities who are happier than some people who are perfectly healthy and fit.

Happy folks have created a sense of joy and purpose for themselves by seeing challenges, not limits. They overcome moments of discouragement and disappointment by taking stock and utilizing what they do have.

It's like the old story of the man who was in the hospital after being in a terrible car wreck. He was in a body cast from his neck to his knees. His comment was, "Yeah, but I can still wiggle my toes!" That was his attitude about his situation. He still could say, "Hey, I'm enjoying this much of it!" No amount of hard luck could take that great attitude away from him, and it was his best asset at that time. What it takes to rebound from a bad situation is to assess your attitude first and see if it serves you in your situation. Afterward work on correcting the problem. This is not a simple task, as health issues can mean discomfort, stress, and debt. Dealing with illness is a difficult experience. However, as Crysalis says, "As long as there is breath there's hope." Understanding illness is half the battle. If your symptoms are bad, you may feel terrible. You are not. Illness does not alter the fact that you are inherently good. No matter how rotten you feel you are still a wonderful human, sacred and worthy. Too often illness alters our self esteem and sense of worth, leaving us feeling guilty and blaming ourselves. There is a difference between taking responsibility for yourself and beating yourself up emotionally. Guilt and blame resolve nothing.

One time I was laid up in bed for three weeks. I did not have the energy to move. Instead of getting caught up with my limitations I began looking for ways to enjoy my time. I ended up finishing a manuscript I had been working on and hadn't found time to complete before.

What could have been a potentially negative experience turned into a writer's coup. You do what you can whatever your limits are. By keeping as active and positive as you can—whatever your situation—you will be able to prove to yourself that happiness can be the best medicine.

HELPFUL TIPS FOR STAYING HAPPY

I believe in treating myself, and in giving myself treats. I deserve them. I don't understand people who always say "I don't deserve it" when someone tries to give them something, whether it is a compliment or a gift. If they keep telling people they don't deserve anything, people will start to believe them.

I love to tell the story of a young lady in the Bear Tribe who, when she was about six, came into a room full of fresh-baked cookies. Now I knew she had already had a couple, and her mother had told her that was enough. She wasn't happy with that, so she waited until I was alone in the room with the cookies. She came in and asked me if she could have one. I asked her why she should have another when mom had said that's enough. She looked at me and said, seriously, "Because I deserve it." She got her cookie.

I like to encourage people to treat themselves. Too often people will play the waiting game with themselves about getting anything they want. They'll tell themselves they can't have something they enjoy until. . . . Often, until doesn't come. Since I feel it is important to treat or reward yourself regularly, I want to suggest some healthy ways to do this. I am not talking about twelve packs of chocolate chip cookies and a gallon of ice cream. I am talking about doing nice, positive things that lighten up your day and let you know you appreciate yourself. Even if you are at a point where you don't think you're a good deserving human being, try some of these tips and you might change your mind about yourself.

1. Get a massage.
2. Get a manicure or a pedicure. Yes men, even you. Get a shoe shine if that makes you more comfortable. Yes women, even you.
3. Buy yourself a present. There can be a broad range here, but be sure to buy what is affordable.
4. Have a head-to-toe herb wrap.
5. Get a hair cut, a perm, or a new hairdo.
6. When the season permits, rake a big pile of leaves together. Jump in them, play with them, throw them up in the air. Rerake them and jump again. Let your laughter and glee surface. Ask your neighbors (who are by now standing in their yard looking at you like you're a little bit nuts, and with a little envy) to join you. You'll be surprised at the response you might get and the fun you'll have. By the way, initially make a big fluffy pile until you gauge your comfortable cushion level and remember, you do land a little harder than when you were a kid.
7. Take a hot bubble bath. Keep on hand a variety of bubble bath products, herbs, fragrances, and bath salts so that you have something special for every mood. Get a tub toy like a rubber ducky, boat, or whale that squirts water. Have a friend join you. Invite them to bring their toys, too. Massage your own or your friends feet. (This can be done in or out of the tub.)
8. If available, take a sauna or whirlpool.
9. Hug a tree.
10. Get a facial.
11. Go to a river. Sit on the bank or walk on the river's edge. Skip rocks, collect pretty rocks and driftwood, sail toy boats (store one in the trunk of your car so when the mood hits you're ready), ponder life, go for a swim, bring bread to feed the ducks or fish, read a book. Bring your dog.
12. Go to the zoo.
13. Have a hot cup of tea. Sit down and really relax while you drink it.
14. Play with your pets.
15. Play with kids. They know lots of ways to relax and have fun. Observe and participate.
16. Take time to be with kids. Let them talk to you. Really listen,

don't interrupt. If allowed to become comfortable, a child can share some of the most profound, beautiful, funny, and sweet things that humans can voice. Being privy to these kinds of conversations can be very relaxing and enjoyable.

17. On the other hand if you have been couped up with your own children for too long, hire a babysitter and escape for an adult activity that gives you privacy, space, and pleasure away from the homefront.

18. Play sports. Basketball, tennis, racketball, badminton, baseball, etc. Play for fun and don't get caught up in competition.

19. Go to the movies. If you have a video machine, rent your favorite movie. Make a big bowl of popcorn. Try low-sodium soya sauce on it and it will be non-fattening and fun.

20. Roast chestnuts. Roast them in the oven if you don't have an open fire. Sing Christmas carols. Do this in August as well as during the holidays just for the silliness of it.

21. Rent a sensual room at a hotel or "bed and breakfast" with someone you like and swing from the chandelier (in a manner of speaking, that is). Have a great time, act out a secret fantasy with a willing partner, bring sexy music and a tape player. If you drink, have a nice bottle of wine, or some delicious juice. Bring long-stemmed glasses—it's the way you serve it that's as important as the content. Bring something sexy to wear, then hardly wear it (this pertains to both men and women). Pack lotion and massage each other. Bring a picnic basket of sensual foods, such as grapes, peaches, chocolate or carob-covered strawberries, and finger foods (finger foods being those that will make you want to lick your own and each others fingers).

22. Work and/or play with your hands: Woodworking, bead-work, knitting, sculpting, drawing, leatherwork, macrame, crocheting, pottery, painting, or candlemaking.

23. Have a heart-to-heart talk with someone you care about. If they live far away, pick up the phone.

24. Play musical instruments and have a sing-a-long. Sentinel Bear keeps a whole variety of musical instruments readily available and encourages others to try this too. He also knows a song for any occasion or event. It's hard to be down in the dumps when you're singing and strumming. He's testimony to that.

25. Go to the theater or a local play.

26. Plant a vegetable and/or flower garden.
27. Cooking can be very relaxing and the results are a fun and delicious bonus. If cooking seems like drudgery, crank up the stereo with your favorite tunes, and try out some decadent recipe that drips off the page of your favorite cookbook.
28. If you hate to cook, go to a wonderful restaurant and order something that drips off the menu.
29. Go to a concert.
30. Go sailing, skiing, bike riding, or roller skating.
31. Play a game.
32. Make a delicious, outrageous basket of food and go on a picnic with good friends, family, or a lover.
33. Make your own list of helpful happy hints. Read it and over a period of time keep adding to it. Watch it grow.
34. Ask your friends what makes them happy. At a party make it a game. People will have fun just talking about what's fun for them.

4 | Sex, Love, and the Life Force

The Creator put us on the earth, and the Creator knows exactly the kind of beings we are. He gave us all the urges and feelings we experience, including those that happen when a man and a woman come together. When you embrace another person and feel an energy surging, you are feeling what the Creator put in you. This is the juice and part of the joy of life. It is okay to feel and enjoy the energy that flows between two people.

When someone sees me embracing a woman they may say, "Well, look at that horny old Sun Bear." My huggee and I don't care because we're feeling good. This energy is perfectly fine; in fact it's sacred. To anyone who doesn't see this I say, "You check it out, acknowledge that it's your problem and deal with it." Because I don't have a problem with sex. I'm happy.

I feel that sexuality is a good energy when we look at it in a sacred manner. Look at nature. Have you ever seen a guilty squirrel? When you look at nature and all of creation around you, you'll see other living beings doing what is natural, and what they have been doing for thousands of years.

The same energy that runs through us and excites us runs through all of life. This energy is the reason grass grows tall and releases little grass seeds so that life begins anew. It is what inspires eagles to dance in mid-air and be playful and wild; twisting and turning; falling, falling; intent on their mating dance; then, at the last moment, releasing their grasp to rise above and fly high into the sky, free and fulfilled.

Look at the corn and see the tassles weave back and forth. All this is like sexual energy, and it is sacred, beautiful, and good. If there isn't new life there aren't new crops. The cycle must continue and the circle must go round and round.

The Navaho people speak of heavy rains as the *He* rains and gentle rains as *She* rains. Throughout their whole culture they acknowledge the male and female energy, the natural forces, as do most tribal people.

When a Canadian Indian sits down at a fire with a woman, they call that sharing power. He is sharing power with that woman. When they come together sexually, they call that sharing power also. If a man and a woman come together at the right time of the month, blending the male and female energy, they bring forth new life. New life is also that same energy you feel when you come together and make love. If you learn how to use that energy you can draw it up through your body and it draws your own energy up. If I don't have any energy and I need to recharge, sometimes I just go out by myself and run my hands over my body and just feel my male energy and bring myself alive with it. Then I have that energy and can use it to transmit healing to somebody. I put my hands on someone and she can feel energy coming from me. That's the life force, the living energy that is in all creation.

The term the Indians of Mexico use to refer to this is "kipura." When they see someone who has a lot of sexual energy in her they say "That person has real kipura." That's a natural force in the person.

Among some tribes the medicine people were picked by the amount of sexual energy they demonstrated. If they had abundant sexual energy, it indicated that the person would have enough energy to make a good medicine man or medicine woman. It expressed tremendous life force, the energy they would need to run ceremonies, to do sweatlodge, and perform the other duties of medicine people.

KEEPING THE LIFE FORCE ALIVE
Many of the healers of other tribal cultures are like this too, both men and women. The older medicine women in their seventies and eighties are frequently seen with young men. The powerful energy of these women keeps them alive and beautiful.

I know medicine men in their eighties who have young women

with them with whom they get along very well on all levels. One medicine brother, who passed on after his ninety-fourth birthday, had the year before fathered a baby with his mate, a young woman.

These older medicine people are of the time of Waboose, the time of the elders, but they keep that youthful energy alive. It is the life force within them. If you learn to work with it when you're younger, and you maintain it, then in your seventies and eighties you'll still be feeling that life force. You'll be feeling alive and acknowledging it.

Many of the native people who are old timers are still very active in all ways. There is an old medicine man up in South Dakota who is in his eighties. A young woman came by to see me who recently had been visiting him. I said, "How's my old friend?" She said, "That old man, he chased me around the table!" "Well," I replied, "I guess he's still okay and in good shape then."

In Canada there is a 100-year-old medicine man. Originally, he was from the Southwest. One night he didn't return and his people thought he was lost. They said, "Where's Grandfather?" They looked everywhere but he couldn't be found. They slept badly that night, being fearful for his safety.

The next morning he arrived home just in time for breakfast with a nice young woman on his arm and a happy smile on his face. He said, "Family, don't worry about me. I'm happy, healthy, and horny!" This elder honored the fires of life that still burned for him, and he was pleased and content.

Among the native people some tribes had what they called a "fire woman." When a young man came to the age where he began to be interested in his sexual energies, this older "fire woman" would come into his life. She would teach him how to make love. She would show him how to experience and work with his sexual energies. He would learn how to respect and work with this life force.

In these tribes there were also older "fire men" who would teach a young girl who had come to an age where she wanted to learn these things. When she was ready, she would spend a year or more with this "fire man." He would teach her about the sacred love force and life force, and how to work with it.

Only people very respected in the tribe could become "fire men or women." Theirs was a position of great and sacred responsibility.

CELEBRATING NEW LIFE

Sexuality was very much a part of tribal culture. In the majority of the ceremonies of native American people this life force is acknowledged as a part of these ceremonies. We especially honor sexuality during the time of earth renewal and the return of the Father Sun. Traditionally, we celebrate this ceremony at the winter solstice.

At this time, all the fires in our lodges are put to sleep. Then, in a ceremonial manner, the flames are reignited. Rekindling the fire represents the return of the Father Sun. From this begins the whole ceremonial year of the native people. It is the time for honoring the fire of life and the flame that burns in and between each of us.

The earth renewal also represents the bringing forth of new life symbolized by the warming of the Earth Mother with the light force of the Father Sun. Since if that doesn't happen none of us will be here, this ceremony is very important.

Tribes of the Southwest have sacred dances they do which honor this time of renewal and the male/female life force energy. In one of the dances a man wears a very long wooden penis and dances around and behind the female dancers in acknowledgement of fertility. The squash-blossom necklaces of Southwestern people, usually made from turquoise and silver, represent fertility, new life, and female sexual energy. These are the ways of my people.

Many of you readers come from a European background. At one time the Celts and other tribal people over there had ceremonies. They did the earth renewal ceremonies, and they danced around in circles, and often times they did ceremonies naked in acknowledgment of their male and female energy, and the blending of that energy into all of life. This blending creates new life. If there wasn't new life there weren't any new crops.

When European tribal people could do these dances around a circle then they had power over their lives. They didn't need to build cathedrals. But new immigrants came to Europe from the dry areas of the Sahara Desert and Asia, and brought a man-, rather than earth-centered religion. They murdered 9 million European people to stop these old religions, the ones that acknowledged the mother, the female energy, and the natural forces. Now we are beginning to come to a point where human consciousness is moving back to female energy. The earth is crying out very loudly, and the herbalists are springing up. Women are becoming healers again. That energy is coming back.

SIN IS IN THE EYE OF THE BEHOLDER

We must still contend with the original European immigrants to America and the changes their twisted views about sexuality have wrought on tribal customs. It is sad what the missionaries brought and what they took away with their Christian teachings and their fears of our native ways. A lot of respect for and knowledge of some of our ceremonies are gone. Much of our heritage was destroyed or made illegal to practice when the white man came and settled. Women were told to cover their breasts and that it was bad and sinful to expose themselves in this manner, despite the fact that some indian women had been going without anything on their breasts for thousands of years and living in peace and harmony. The only sin was in the missionary's head and heart. They were having problems looking at those nice brown-breasted maidens. The tribal people honored their bodies and were not offended by their natural beauty. They accepted the natural forces. They were at peace with their sexual energies, and with the female energy in all its manifestations.

THE MOON TIME

Traditionally tribal women came together to dance at the time of the full or new moon, and when they were menstruating, which we refer to as the moon time. During moon time some of the women would go off by themselves and release some of their blood on the earth. This is an acknowledgment of nurturing from the Earth Mother and of their womanhood, beauty, and power, which reflect the energy of the earth. Dancing a sacred dance is a way of giving a gift back to the Earth Mother.

Women have told me that dancing with the earth beneath them and the night sky above them has helped to relieve the pain of premenstrual syndrome, if they dance just before their moon time. Any woman who wants to can do this now. Dance and feel the earth beneath you. Release the energies that are constricting you. A lot of the energies that women feel during their moon time go back to the beginning of creation. These are creative energies.

When a woman ovulates, it is a good time for her to go out and draw the energy of the earth into her. To do this, feel the energy from the Mother come up through the ground into your being and acknowledge this power that she gives you.

Many female health problems originate from repression. Women are conditioned with large doses of nice girl/bad girl propoganda. They are taught to be afraid to feel their female energies, so these energies pull back. It is no wonder health issues arise.

I encourage women—and men—to watch animals. Observe how the birds fly free, their motion fluid, gliding, and sensual. Each does their own sky dance on wings spread wide, moving on the currents of air, and flying a pattern all their own. Notice how animals stretch, hunt, move, run, sleep, and eat dominated only by their instinctual needs. Are there ways you can learn and integrate some of the freedom of motion your sisters and brothers of the animal kingdom have? Yes: watch them and let them teach you.

Some animals mate for life like the wolf and the eagle. Others run wild, mating when their instincts spur them on. Nature sings her gentle song to them. Their life force energy flows. The physical being prepares for the dance where two become one. Unity. The cycle of life manifests itself through the physical plane; the circle is complete; life begins afresh.

FINDING A NATURAL RHYTHM

Like animals, people also have a natural rhythm. Some human beings are monogamous and others are not. Some choose to bear children, others do not. How you maintain your sexuality should be done in balance with what your needs are, what kind of person you are, and with respect for those with whom you choose to have relations.

These are challenging times for those humans who have various sexual mates, but there are many ways to have "safe sex," especially with the use of condoms. I wholeheartedly encourage this for any persons who are not in a long-term monogamous relationship. And for those who don't want the responsibilities of parenting children, there are a variety of forms of birth control available.

I think it is important to enjoy your sensuality, the expression of your loving, sexual being. How you express yourself is really up to you and your partner. Anything can be fine as long as you enjoy it and are using safe-sex basics. I leave personal options up to people and try not to place my limitations or preferences on others.

We frequently have had visitors at The Bear Tribe or students at my programs who would ask me how I felt about different sexual preferences. My reply usually is, "What a person does with another consenting adult is between them. Everyone is welcome to agreeably work out whatever they want with whomever they want, as long as both parties are in full agreement."

If you are not in touch with your sexual energy or if you deny this life force, you can create definite imbalances for yourself. Sure, there are times in everyone's life where energy is focused in other areas and sexuality is not a priority. However, if the urge is never there or if the urge is there but your body won't cooperate, then it is important to investigate the cause and take measures to correct this. Usually the problem stems from an energy block. These blocks may be a result of physical problems, of improper nutrition, or of mental or emotional distress.

Mental or emotional blocks can come from early childhood problems. Certain conditionings of this society teach that sexuality is sinful. A negative or abusive experience, or simply repressed energy can also cause these blocks.

Frequently, people give up their personal control over their lives. They give away their freedom to choose their own belief systems and allow others to dictate their lives and what is right or wrong for their bodies. The direct result of this can be sexual malfunctioning. It is difficult for someone who is living with tremendous guilt to really relax and enjoy sex.

When dealing with your own sexuality the first thing you need to understand is that you have a right to your own natural life force energy, as long as you respect the rights of others. You have a right to be alive. You have a right to be loved and to enjoy contact with other human beings. It doesn't always have to be sexual intercourse. An embrace can be very loving and powerful. If it is very difficult for you to be touched, a massage can be a safe way to help you open up and get beyond your untouchable feelings. If you feel you are unattractive, body image work with a therapist can help you to appreciate your own special qualities. Finding out that it is okay to explore yourself can be a beautiful revelation.

Love yourself enough to take the time to really find out what your personal likes and dislikes are. Find out what you really have to offer and love yourself for it. Then allow yourself to start building a true love relationship with another person. Through such relationships we really touch the sacredness and the vibrant life energy the Creator has placed within all humans. By touching this energy within ourselves we get rid of a lot of the problems that could otherwise keep us from being happy and healthy human beings.

5 | Opening Up to the Universe

To be truly healthy you need to carefully and courageously assess your approach to the universe. The universe is wide open, and full of forces willing to work with us two-leggeds. Yet, most people go through life as if they were ignorant of these forces. They act like they are not really sure where they are going, where they have been, what they're doing, or why. *They are taught to experience only through the brain and not through the senses.* To walk a true spiritual path one must "feel." The greatest tools for opening up to the universe are a sense of awareness, intuition, and the ability to *feel* life and the universe, as it happens, all around you and through you.

Once I was doing a Stone People's Ceremony at a workshop in Alabama. An Episcopalian priest from a large congregation in Atlanta came into my sweatlodge. When he emerged from the lodge, tears were streaming down his face. He took me aside and said, "Sun Bear, that is the first real religion I have *felt* in twenty-five years." He went on to say that he felt conventional religion had become so pasteurized and formalized that its power has dissipated.

Native American teachings and spiritual ways still have their power, in part because they are very individual. In the sweatlodge, you are sweating and praying. In the pipe ceremony, you are holding the pipe, smoking, and sending your voice in prayer. At the Medicine Wheel Gatherings you make the tobacco ties, sing, and spend time at the places of the wheel that draw you. If you have thirty-six stones you can make a medicine wheel at home and work with those energies anytime. Smudging can be done on a daily basis whenever you feel it is appropriate, as can several other ceremonies I'll describe in chapter 9.

One extremely powerful way to open up to the universe is

through the Vision Quest. While I talk about this in detail in chapter 9 I want to share here how powerful a ceremony a Vision Quest can be. Traditionally, it is a time of fasting and praying during which you ask, "How can I best serve the people? How can I best serve the Earth Mother? How can I best serve future generations?" During this time you cry both figuratively and literally for your vision.

The Cheyenne dog soldiers were people who knew how to cry for vision, and how to serve their people. They were great warriors on all levels. In battle a dog soldier would tie a rope around his waist and peg the other end into the ground. He would not retreat. He fought until all the enemy or he himself greeted death. A dog soldier would say, "Remember the children, remember the old ones, and remember the helpless ones. We do this so that the people might live."

Today, if your path guides you to be a spiritual warrior—one who will help the people to live—and you want to walk the sacred road, you should not carry a gun or a bow and arrow. You need tools and knowledge to protect yourself and your people. With these you create, build, and expand your circle of energy in a spiritual manner. You should protect your heart not by carrying a shield but by carrying the ancient song of the people in your breast. The true spiritual warrior gives of his life so that the people might live.

ALL CREATION HAS LIFE

To native people all creation has life in it. Learning how to feel that life opens you up to learn about the universe and all it has to offer. Nature is not dumb. Humanity is dumb when we can't hear or when we forget how to communicate with nature. Nature is very much alive. Intelligent living beings and vibrant energies are all over the planet.

Want to prove this to yourself? With a willing partner, place the palms of your hands about four inches from the palms of your partner's hands. Feel the energy. Slowly move your hands back and forth. Feel the energy build. It may feel like a tingling, heat or cold, like a gentle tension, or like a thickness in the air between your palms. Slowly continue to move your hands while feeling the energy change and grow. Next, take a moment to hug your partner. Really feel the energy that passes between you. Don't you feel more alive?

After doing this, go outside and find a tree you like and hug it. And I mean hug it! Give it a good dose of love, with abandon. Take time to let the tree respond. Feel the energy the tree sends back to you. It may be different every time you do this exercise. It's also different with varied species of trees. While you are outdoors you can also lay out flat on the ground and hug the Earth Mother. Feel the love and nurturing she sends back.

These are a few ways to begin to feel the life and unique individuality of all the parts of our universe, starting with the Earth Mother. Remember, when you begin this path you see just a little twinkle of the energy of the universe, but when you devote yourself to it you see a whole sky full of brilliant stars.

There are many dynamic and powerful energies in the universe. Different spiritual people work with these elements in different ways. In some ceremonies there is a great respect for exactness; in others, for creativity. For those beginning to practice ceremony it is good to be precise or a variety of unexpected things might result. The ceremony could be less powerful than it would be if it were done exactly. If it is a healing ceremony, the healing might not take place. In a rain-making ceremony, the rain might not come. If you are working with certain spirit elements and offend them, you may not be prepared for the consequences. So it is important to follow a traditional ceremony with precision and respect.

I have an apprentice who wasn't doing her groundwork or following the sacred guidelines her teachers laid out for her. She had the idea she was going to be very powerful and so spent all her time praying in a manner that I call "pounding on the doors of heaven." She always wanted to be the biggest, the bravest, and suffer the most for her path. She was a real overachiever in all the wrong ways. One night she was doing a ceremony in her apartment when a tremendous whirlwind came in. Even though her doors and windows were closed and fastened, papers were flying around and things were coming off the walls and bookshelves. Well, she completely freaked out. She ran out the door, found a phone, and called me long distance. She said, "Sun Bear, Sun Bear, this terrible thing is happening," and she explained what had taken place. I replied, "Well, it didn't hurt you, or kill you did it? Why didn't you ask it what it wanted?" Remember this story as you walk your path. As you reach for health and knowledge you are reaching for sacred power as well. Be ready for it.

I have another apprentice who is a young man who can be extremely arrogant. I let his own arrogance teach him his needed lesson. He stepped out of line a bit too often and the other people in the apprentice program jumped all over him about it. When he stopped his nonsense, his relationship with the group became very positive, which was good reinforcement for him. From that honest place he began to feel his own true being, who he actually was.

He discovered he liked his true self better than his arrogant self. He felt alive and vibrant. After these revelations he really began to feel the ceremonies we did. He connected deeply with the Earth and real change began to happen. He's gotten so he comes back for a workshop every so often just to check his circuits and get honest feedback about his behavior. This helps him to keep himself on track so he does not fall back into his old ways.

"INSTANT HOLIES"

Many people are anxious for power but they don't bother to take the time to find out what it's really about. They settle for much less in the long run because they never have the knowledge or respect that can create the truest and purest of powers. Learning through practice and patience to reach for things in a sacred manner is very important.

Often, people who come to workshops looking for power are actually souvenir collectors. They say, "Well, this week I'm going to see Sun Bear, next week I'm going to see Guru Chi Chi." They get nothing from any workshop because they don't know how to discriminate and find their own path.

People come to me and ask, "What is your thing? What can you do for me?" I say, "I can't teach you. I can only teach those who are willing to take responsibility, to integrate and own the knowledge of the spiritual warrior. I only teach those who walk the spiritual path because they want to help with the problems in the world, help heal the earth mother, and help take care of their brothers and sisters. I teach those who want to take in the sacred knowledge and use it in everyday life to make a difference."

I walk around people if I don't feel I can help them or if they are not ready for my help. I don't wear myself out over them. I would never go out of my way to hurt anyone, but I don't try to rescue anybody either. I have had to develop this attitude because some people are so eager for a power rush they want to run off a spiritual cliff to get it. *There is no fast, easy way.* There are no "instant holies." People have come to learn from me who have different medicine from mine and I've told them to pursue other paths. If you are truly feeling your way along your path then that will be enough. You will find some of the many different ways of opening up to the universe.

Life is moving at an ever-accelerating pace so you are going to have to dance a little faster. What you learn—your knowledge— becomes your tools, your sacred weapons with which to do battle. These tools fortify you so you are no longer a victim, so you can break free from human conditioning and truly make a difference in your life.

One interesting avenue for some people is that of past lives. As you open up to the universe you may begin to connect with other lifetimes you have lived. Once I met a woman at a gathering who said she wanted to talk to me. She said she had been my wife in a past life when I was a Mongolian chief who led many warriors. She described something to see if I would remember it. What she described were all scenes I had seen before. I remembered all that had happened and realized these were events that had come from my dreams. She told me about an area in northern China. It was a village at war. There were many tents. At least 100 warriors waving torches bore down in a fierce attack. As she closed her tale our eyes met and a bond of old was renewed. Our paths may cross again in this lifetime or the next. However, I was grateful for the chance to reaffirm and reunite with my past in my present.

Spirit has reminded me of the time before I came into this world as Sun Bear. I was somewhere in the universe that was nothing like earth. I was observing my life-to-be. I had to choose the identity with which I would live, from what seemed like a triple soul bank available to me. My choices were to come in as Sun Bear, as an El Salvadorian, or as a black man in Chicago. I am happy with the choice I made. It feels right to me. My sacred path has been a good teacher to me, a growing experience. Life has taught me to really embrace my power.

SPIRITS ANSWER

I've traveled all over the world working with different people and shamans from all walks of life and sacred paths. No matter where ceremony is done, when the spirits are called, they answer. In different parts of the world different names are used for the spirit forces, but they are the same ancient powers that have been in effect in the universe for all of time.

When I was in Guatemala, a group of us did ceremony alongside a lake and three big volcanos. We prepared prayer feathers and other offerings. We brought them down to the lake, which was very calm. After placing them in the earth we started praying. Immediately, waves began churning all over the lake, and lapping all around our feet and over the offerings. I said, "Hey, the spirits are hungry for these offerings."

It is this way all over the world. This medicine works wherever I go. Friends of mine in Germany like to bring me from one power spot to another because they want to see what will happen. They brought me to what is called the "Big Dream Rocks," and immediately the wind went from being calm to billowing currents of air.

When Crysalis was doing a crystal mining event in Lake Tahoe, the weather had been very sunny and clear. On the afternoon I was arriving, the sky clouded up and it began to rain. Crysalis looked up at the sky and said, "Sun Bear is almost here, it's beginning to rain. There always seem to be weather changes when Sun Bear arrives." These are some of the ways the elemental forces respond and show their presence.

In Hawaii, the elements are particularly strong because the people are still working, blending, and connecting with the land and elements. They open up to the universe in their own special way with ceremonies which have been handed down through generations of Kahunas. They have powers which have been given to them directly from the forces of the universe. The Kahunas are a powerful people who do extremely potent ceremony.

Working with the elements in Hawaii was like nothing I had ever experienced before. I would begin to pray and call in a spirit force and in an instant the force would be there. The Kahunas liked to watch me do ceremony. On one occasion, we went to a place where we had previously built a ceremonial Medicine Wheel. Our focus, on this occasion, was on the need for rain. I made preparations and then began the sacred pipe ceremony. About half way through the ceremony my eyes were drawn to the sky. Looming above us were two enormous thunderclouds. They looked close to opening the skies and letting rain pour down. I raised my eagle feather and on the opposite side of the valley two twin rainbows appeared. I said, "Please Brother Thunderbeings, not yet." Then I completed the pipe cermony and said, "Everyone, take cover quickly." The second after we got under shelter, lightning filled the skies and the clouds opened, releasing torrential rain. The earth was happy that day for she received a much needed drink from the sky brothers.

Another day, we went to King Kamehameha's Temple of the Shark to do ceremony. I did a pipe facing the ocean. Immediately, the water broke and became alive with sharks. There were 150 to 200 sharks out there. About one-half mile beyond them a whale surfaced. All during the time I was praying, the whale was hitting the water with his tail just like he was beating a drum for the ceremony. I finished the ceremony and he swam away. I really feel love for that powerful old whale.

Another time, I did a Medicine Wheel on the big island of Hawaii. There were about 1,500 people there. I prayed with my pipe and asked that the forces be with us. The next morning the volcano erupted.

We took a picture of the volcano and the eruption in the photo looks like the outline of a woman with her arms in the air. I was told this is Pele, the goddess of the volcano, showing herself to us. They say that the same image of the goddess shows herself at times to the Kahunas, usually in the clouds, making the image in the photo familiar to many Hawaiians.

The Kahunas have been working with the forces for thousands of years. The results are everywhere on these lush islands where the most beautiful flowers, exotic plants, and delicious fruits in the world can be found. The Kahunas have a close connection with the plant, animal, and ocean life. The volcanos, monsoons, hurricanes, and tropical storms are just a few of the elements with which the Kahunas have deep and powerful relationships. They help to maintain a precious balance in this beautiful paradise. Many Kahunas can be gentle, loving, and caring people. But do not foolishly anger them, nor ever ridicule their power. Even the park rangers give them full respect, restraining tourists from visiting their private ceremonial areas. For when these people call in the powers, things happen.

"SPIRIT STUFF"

The spirit forces are all around us. They are constantly showing themselves to me and to others who willingly open themselves to the universe.

On many occasions, kinetic events have happened where pictures fall off walls, glasses jump off tables, books fall off shelves, etc. One day I was lying down. My eyes were drawn to my suitcase on the floor. The strap that kept it fastened when I traveled lay across it. While I watched, the strap rose up in the air and then lay back down.

Years ago, I was having a brief moment of reflection, pondering all this "spirit stuff." I had just come to the conclusion that it was all baloney when the door opened and shut by itself. I said, "Oh yes, I got it." At some point, you just see too many things you can't explain and you have to know there is some power or force behind them.

I have watched these powers and forces for many years now. I have watched them in my own work, and I have watched them in the work of many other people who have gifts of power for which there is absolutely no explanation—scientific or otherwise. These forces have always been here, but civilization has shunned them. Now the people are calling to them, and they are responding and coming back.

Getting in touch with these forces is an ongoing process. We are constantly learning. I feel mankind is trying not to get lost along the way and when we get off course, we consistently try to pull ourselves back on track. At this time in history we have gone off course. A supreme effort must be made to get back on a track healthy for our race and for the Earth Mother.

If we can not accomplish this ourselves, then the Earth Mother will find a way to cleanse us from her as she does her self-healing.

Humanity's progress is like a group of people going over a great hill. With each wave of people a certain number of them make it over the top of that hill. Then they pray that the next wave makes it over the hill. It is like the old theory of taking the hand of the person moving in front of you and offering your other hand to the person behind you. The rule is that you are responsible for yourself. If you don't live your life in complete and impeccable integrity to the best of your ability, you remove yourself from this chain.

There are many different forces and powers in the universe. With each wave of humanity we struggle to reach and maintain a level of goodness and to keep evil at bay. That's why reaching a higher level of consciousness is important. Higher consciousness gives you the strength to climb that great hill. It's a way to create the force that aligns you with the course God and the spirits have set for you. No one can do this for you. We can encourage you and give you some pointers along the way, but you have to get there by yourself. This is because Spirit is interested in people developing consciousness from a free will, from making a choice because they want to make it. That's the bottom line. When your choices are a willing gift, you begin to perfect your consciousness.

When I started my teaching path Great Spirit said, "Don't draw people to you out of panic by emphasizing the earth changes. Let them come from a want for higher knowledge and because they have come to the conclusion that this is a sacred path. Let them come because they want to serve their fellow human beings in a sacred manner."

A DIFFERENT DANCE
When I was working at Indian reservations, people came to me from the local churches and dropped off boxes of old clothes that their parish people donated, although they were too worn out to be of any use. Time and again there would be just one shoe or one sock. These folks must have thought there were an awful lot of one-legged Indians around. I began to really think about why they would send these boxes of beat up and unusable clothes. I realized, they weren't doing it for me or the other Indians or for love of a fellow human being or because they wanted to help. They weren't doing it just to be nice. They did it to earn brownie points from the Sky Gods to help them get out of going to hell or guarantee them a trip into heaven.

You have to do things in life because you want to, because you enjoy what you are doing and you believe in it. That is the point of the dance of life. It can't be because you get a little stroke from God. This is the truth of the sacred dance. The more completely you can come from this place of choice, the more completely you will open yourself to the full power of the universe.

All that we do is sacred. Every choice and decision is sacred. We must always choose truthfully from a place of personal integrity. The sacred teachings say the people going into the next world will carry the law within their heart. You cannot go through life making choices because someone is swinging a billy club over your head. You have to do it from your heart because you want to. The next world isn't going to have any policemen or babysitters, or mommies or daddies. You won't get to that world if you rely on other people in this lifetime. It is an altogether different dance. Rid yourself of the beliefs within you that require someone to keep them in balance every step of the way.

Everyday I try to reach out to my brothers and sisters on their level, without judging their dance at that moment. I give people what they need when I can. I don't take responsibility for everything and I don't mourn the whole world. In the apprentice program, I'll give you a pat on the shoulder, a kick in the rear, and a variety of other things, but I won't do the program for you. You are the one who has to formulate your values and principles. You need to integrate the knowledge and learn how to use what is given to you.

One person came to the Bear Tribe and plopped himself down on my doorstep. He said, "My life is a mess, Sun Bear. Will you fix it for me?" I said, "No! It's your mess. You made it, you need to fix it."

Opening up to the universe and becoming a spiritual warrior allows you to go to any level in this society. It's important to know how to make things happen instead of waiting for them to happen. The idea is to grow into a level of power where you can look at any aspect of the world and have no fear, where you know how to undo the knots in life and not cry over not being able to solve the world's problems. I encourage these attitudes in everyone I work with. I want them to be my spiritual playmates. I want them to have the power, consciousness, and ability to move around the universe working and playing in a sacred manner. The core of people I'm working with are moving at a high level and pace of consciousness that is conducive to making things happen in the universe.

Now is the time for this to happen, because our whole system, as we know it, is moving into oblivion. It's a time of making a choice to be part of the solution and embrace the light, or sink into the dark. The responsibility of the forces that have been here for thousands of years is to work with humankind. Once you are connected with the powers, it is your responsibility to work with humankind also.

If you are just going along living your life, going from your TV to work, just existing, then these forces aren't going to bother with you because you don't bother them. You aren't asking for anything and they don't come looking for you. You have got to go looking for them.

We all come to this planet equal. We all come from our Mother's womb and here we are. Then we make a choice. It can happen or not. We can just exist and that is fine because no one is going to demand much of you. Or we can "pry open the bales" and find out there is something very real and powerful out there and inside of each of us. Now is the time to connect with your higher powers, spirit guardians, and spirit forces and cry for your vision. Go to them and say, "Hey, I am dumb!" Cry for knowledge. Let the forces know that you know there is something out there and you want some of it. That is when the forces come to you. They say, "Oh, somebody is looking for us," and then the dance begins.

6 | Eat Your Way to Health and Longevity

Traditionally native American people lived long, happy, healthy, and balanced lives. They ate wholesome, fresh, and natural food. They got up with the sun and went to bed with the moon. Through the natural course of their lives of hunting and living in nature they got a lot of exercise every day. They did everything in a respectful way to honor the balance of life, Mother Earth, and Great Spirit. Through ceremony they showed their gratitude to the earth and all their relations upon her.

In general, the native American people were celebrators of life. Because they loved and respected life, many of them lived long fruitful lives. Those who died young often did so because of battle, physical injury, or accident. Many parts of native philosophies provide the key to living to a ripe old age. True purpose, positive attitude, good health habits, and a connection with nature and the Creator are some of the key factors in living past your eighties and nineties into your hundreds.

I have a friend named Don Jose who is a spiritual teacher in Mexico. He is healthy, active, and happy at nearly 110 years old. His wife is nearly ninety years old and bore her last child at sixty-five. She was married when she was fourteen years old and now is the mother of twelve children. She is well known for getting up at gatherings and dancing their sacred deer dance in a spry and happy manner.

They live by the formula of balancing physical work, a simple diet, ceremony, and humor. Their diet is primarily corn, beans, vegetables, and a little chicken. They work their fields, grow their own crops, and acquire good physical exercise in the process. The key to their longevity is they enjoy every moment and do what they believe in. They completely respect the cycle, the balance, and the ceremonies of their lives. Everything they need is there.

Many of the Hopi people in the Southwest live to be 80, 90, or 100 years old. Their philosophy is, "You do whatever you are able to do for as long as you are able to do it." When a man is in his seventies or eighties, he still has a cornfield to hoe that is located about ten miles from his village. When he gets too old to do that, then he starts hoeing the cornfield that is only five miles from the village. When he can't hoe any longer, he weaves. The Hopis are active and they stay active. They continually take their part of the work, the ceremony, and the fun. They have a sense of being an important part of the universe all of the time. By living their lives and staying a part of the cycle of life, they know they are helping to maintain the universe.

Sentinel Bear's maternal grandmother of Polish descent was determined to live to be 100 years old. She passed on shortly after she celebrated being on this earth for a century. Her formula for longevity was to keep a good sense of humor, to not "sweat the small stuff," to cherish her good relationship with God, and to remain busy, saying rosaries and shaking her crochet hook with the best of them to the very end! She was a wonderful woman, loved by many, mainly because she wasn't afraid to be either wonderful or loving.

I know two brothers who were medicine men up in Minnesota. They lived to be 120 years old. They'd get out and chop their wood, carry water, and do all the chores on even the coldest winter days. They embraced their lives until the very end.

In my home country, there was a 137-year-old Chippewa man who lived at the Cass Lake Reservation. He remembered Lincoln's inauguration. He had seventeen wives in his lifetime. Some of them died and some of them "split the blanket" and went their own way. But through all of his life he remained active. Unfortunately, one day he took a fall and injured his hip. He was brought to a local hospital, although he was none too pleased about it. His hip was mending nicely. However, the hospital had steam heat to which he was not accustomed. Because of the heat he contracted pneumonia. At 137 years old he died from the pneumonia.

In order to live to an old age, it is important to enjoy life and to feel that you are doing something useful that has some purpose or meaning. You need to have a purpose for living.

I've heard stories about two people who have the same severe illness. One person dies while the other gets well. Almost always these stories say that the person who had the will to live, who enjoyed life or had a meaningful purpose was the one to recover.

The human brain has the capacity to last a long time and with proper care, the body can be very durable. The more you learn to control your brain and the messages sent from your brain to your body, the longer you're going to live. You can extend your time here on earth if you can train your brain, spirit, and body to integrate deeper levels of consciousness through whatever means are most comfortable for you—be they ceremony, prayer, meditation, or anything else that works for you.

THINK YOURSELF YOUNG

Fate always has a hand in any process. However, it is most important to learn how to take the edge in your favor in the ways over which you do have control. Then stop worrying about the areas that you can't do anything about. Do the best you can and let the rest go. Too often we think we should grow old and therefore age before our time. People buy into their own negative conditioning. They say, "Well, I'm fifty years old now and I can't do this and I can't do that. And now I'm sixty years old and I can't do this either. I'm just going to hang it up. Probably even if I am still able to have sex, no one will want to have it with me." Baloney! Too many people today are so busy neutering themselves, they have no idea how much they can do and how much fun it can be to do things at any age.

A fifty-year-old woman came to me a while back and said she was recently widowed, which meant to her no more sex and nothing better to do than knit booties and shawls. Well, I gave her a pep talk that would burn your ears about staying alive, healthy, happy, and horny. I encouraged her to change the conditioning tapes she had been fed by her family and society and not to be so ready to put herself out to pasture. We parted company at that time and she commented that she had a lot to think about.

I saw her six months later and hardly recognized her. She had a new hairdo, a radiant look on her face, and a skip to her walk. She came zipping up to me and said, "Oh Sun Bear, thank you for our conversation. My life has taken on new meaning. I'm traveling places I've never been before. I've started a new career and am dating a nice energetic man who takes me backpacking and fishing." I told her that was good. I asked her when she had time to knit those booties and shawls she told me about. Her reply was, "I don't have time and I don't plan on making the time because I've found a lot of better things to do!"

I invite you to think yourself young, think yourself happy, and think yourself well. You can do your best to deny the conditioning placed on you to grow old long before it's time. To help you do this you should repeat the following sentence, or one similar to it, at least twice a day. Say, "I am going to be around a long time. I am healthy, happy, living a good life, and sexually vibrant, too!" Feel the vitality of the life force. This vitality is our gift from the Great Spirit. Spirit doesn't want us to die either young or apathetically. The Great Spirit wants us to enjoy long happy lives and celebrate them until our last breath.

Life has many twists, so when problems arise, don't hide from them. Don't run from your battles and challenges. Face and fight them with pride. If a lesson is particularly painful, or difficult, remain humble but realize Great Spirit felt you a powerful and deserving enough warrior to give you an important battle.

HUNTING HEALTH AND LONGEVITY
Humans are warriors by nature. For all of time we have done battle, whether on a physical or spiritual level. It is these spiritual battles that have honed us as individuals and helped us to evolve as a society. And contrary to the concept that Great Spirit never gives us more than we can handle, I feel we are often given more than is comfortable, as a catalyst to help us become more than we are. This pressure helps us to grow and evolve beyond ourselves, to peak past our limitations.

The natural warrior in us just loves this. It perks us up and grabs our attention. It's what makes the human spark in us ignite. The idea is to embrace your challenges and rise to the occasion. In such challenging situations, most important of all is that humans discover time and time again they can handle much more than they thought. Humans have a phenomenal ability to stretch beyond their own limits. The key is choice. If we choose to, we can do amazing things we never thought possible.

Sometimes doctors heal people with miracle medicines, and sometimes people heal themselves without any medicines. We go to the moon. Athletes beat unbelievable records over and over again. It comes down again and again to choice. People choose to devote themselves to discovering new medicine. Athletes give themselves totally to their sport. Astronauts beg to touch the stars. These people make conscious decisions about what they want and go for it. Sure, we call these wonders miracles, but all of life is a miracle. In all miracles are elements of choice, planning, and follow through. Choices aren't always pleasant. Those who don't accept the challenges life deals them can and do have a rough time of it. This is where depression, apathy, addiction, unrest, impotence, pain, and all the other unpleasant business comes in.

I'm not saying that everything can be cured with a "snap." It takes the formulation of a plan of action to get from point *A* to point *B*. But you can bank on the fact that if you are not planning action, then nothing is going to happen. In today's world, there is no way out or around, only through.

When my people went out on a hunt they prepared for it, focused on it, planned it, prayed for it, and then went out and did it. If they didn't have a successful hunt they got ready for another one. There were no questions about this. If they hunted, they ate. If they didn't hunt, they starved. The same principle applies today on many levels. However, contemporary people starve emotionally and spiritually more often than they do physically. And they starve in these ways all the time. Go on your personal healing and longevity hunt. Hone your skills. Prepare yourself. Maintain your abilities. Plan your work and work your plan.

If you want to live to be 150, plan on it. Try this simple recipe for a long life that I call "The Everyday Plan." Challenge and stretch your imagination every day. Exercise every day. Follow a good nutritional program everyday. Connect, give thanks, and open yourself to the Creator on some level every day. Do some affirmations and consciously choose a healthy, happy, and joyful attitude every day that will allow you daily satisfaction for however many years you live.

When you have "The Everyday Plan" down, then you are ready to go on to a more refined and complicated rejuvenation plan that has been helpful for me and some of the other people who work with me.

SUN BEAR'S REJUVENATION PROGRAM

This program acknowledges that living to a ripe old age depends a lot upon good nutrition and a structured health plan. It used to be easier to sustain your body's nutrients because the food was cleaner without perservatives or processing. The food chain has been weakened by the misuse of the earth. Since it is difficult to get all the nutrients we need from food, it may be necessary to take vitamins and supplements to restore our balance. Over the years I've put together a rejuvenation program that has worked well for me. I'm at a point now where I know what my imbalances are and I have some tried and true measures I take to get back on track.

A good way to find out what your imbalances are is to be tested by a holistic doctor, chiropractor, herbalist, or nutritionist who specializes in this area. Frequently, everything from colds and recurring infections to despondency and emotional problems can be traced to vitamin deficiencies, or food or environmental allergies.

As a rule of thumb, when I want to cleanse and purify my body or diet, or strengthen my constitution, I have a standard program I follow. I developed this program for myself. Each person's body is different, so eventually you will have to create a program that will be most beneficial to you.

Frequently I do workshops at places where I do not have control over the foods I am served. My constitution can get a little topsy-turvy from this but, as soon as possible, I go to my program and straighten myself out.

It is a little naive to think you are going to be able to go on any program and achieve perfect health, especially if you're approaching your middle or later years. Little aches and pains are bound to surface now and then, but the important thing is not to get too shook up. Instead, use your energy to take the steps that will get you back on course as soon as possible. Keep striving for a youthful, positive attitude that will energize you even if you feel achey. This attitude will get you to the 100-year mark better than anything.

Hopefully, some of what I do will be helpful to you on your road to health. After you decide on what will work for you, consult with your physician to see if it meets with her idea of what is good for you. It is never a good idea to start any dietary or exercise program without first consulting a trusted health care professional.

EAT YOUR WAY TO HEALTH

Every food is sacred. Food is a gift of life from the Earth Mother and Great Spirit. All nourishment that passes your lips is a sacrament. You should honor and respect all that you eat. At the Bear Tribe we form a circle and join hands in prayer before each meal. We give thanks to the Creator for each bit of food that comes to our table, for every meal and for every harvest. Such thanks and honor form the foundation of a healthy diet.

The most important part of your relationship with food comes from your relationship with Spirit. The more respect you have for the cycle of life, for the balance between your needs and nature, the more goodness you will get from your food. Let every bite of food be a prayer of thanks. Celebrate the fact that you are eating by chewing slowly and truly enjoying the taste and texture of your food.

In chapter 1 I told you it is what is eating you—the mind creatures—that set the stage for dis-ease. The food you put into your body can also make a big difference in whether any dis-eases get to play a big role on the stage of your life.

In the old days, my people ate what the earth mother gave them: wild greens and vegetables, roots, herbs, occasional berries, fruits or honey, and wild meat or fish raised without chemicals. The water they drank was pure, and the air was free of pollution.

Later, when some native people began farming, they changed their diet by adding a wider variety of vegetables, particularly the sacred three sisters: corn, beans, and squash, and more fruits and berries. These enabled them to make a wider variety of dishes. But they still did not have anything close to the number of choices or the temptations we have today. White sugar, white flour, salt, and chemicals weren't in everything, and there was no food that had been processed to the point where it had lost its life force. My people did not face water that was not fit to drink and air not fit to breathe.

Those of us living in this day of wide dietary choices have to learn to choose carefully if we want long and healthy lives. While diet is a very personal affair, to make it work for you, you need to think of it as a formula you can design for your own health and happiness.

What follow here are some of my favorite items for health and rejuvenation.

Water

Water is a real priority on my list of top items for good health. You can live without food for weeks, but you can live for only a few days without water.

Water is the main factor in cleansing, purifying, and eliminating wastes from the body. It helps to balance the appetite. It prevents constipation and skin disorders, and helps to keeps your body functioning from "nose to toes!" As a rule, I drink eight to ten glasses of water a day. I always try to drink water that has been through some kind of purification process. Sadly, the water that comes from most taps today is not fit for drinking.

Raw Fruits and Vegetables

A lot of healthy liquid can be gained from vegetables, fruits, and juices. Raw fruits and vegetables are my next highest priority food when I'm working hard to cleanse and purify or heal a particular ailment.

At the Bear Tribe, we now are growing a good part of our food in our Sacred Buffalo Hunt Garden. Simon Henderson (Cornman) is our permaculture expert and master gardener.

Although I travel over 90 percent of the year, I do make it a point to include lots of raw fruits and vegetables as a primary food source. When I get back to our home base in Spokane, Washington, I heavily indulge in all of Simon's delicious, fresh, home-grown, and home-processed vegetables and fruits.

After I have been at a workshop where the food has been of questionable quality or heavily processed, I try to eat only raw vegetables and fruit for a couple of days. My favorites are beets (I eat the leaf and all), celery, carrots, and onions.

I like to have a wide variety of salads, juices, fruit, and vegetable dishes prepared for when I get hungry. This way I have nutritional food available so junk food won't be so tempting. When you do this, use your favorite vegetables and be creative in mixing them together in salads. Also, keep a big fruit salad on hand.

Juices are great for cleansing the system. You can always pick up bottled, all natural fruit juices. However, whenever it's possible, juice your own. When I'm concentrating hard on my rejuvenation program, I'll take a day of just eating raw fruits and drinking fruit juices. This is very purifying and energizing.

Sprouts
Sprouts are a big part of my health program and bring me much life and vitality. Sprouts are nutritional, strengthening, easily digestible, healthy, and healing for all your organs. They help produce energy, clean the system, help elimination, are great for the skin, and are very delicious. I use them on everything I can and eat them as a snack by themselves. You can buy them in a store or sprout them yourself. There are a wide variety of sprouts available beyond the common alfalfa sprout. Try some of these others.

Wheat Grass
Wheat grass is one of the richest natural sources of minerals, calcium, iron, zinc, sodium, phosphorus, potassium, cobalt, magnesium, and vitamins A, B, and C. Wheat grass is known to have antibiotic properties. Juice made from wheatgrass is said to be 70 percent chlorophyll.

It can even be used in your bath to clean the skin and rejuvenate your pores. Wheat grass has been successfully used for toothaches, constipation, and as an overall healer and strengthener. It also has been used to help clear up skin troubles, enhance endurance, reduce high blood pressure, neutralize toxicity in the body, restore vitality, and tone-up the heart, lungs, and female organs. It's said to destroy bacteria, heal scar tissue, and reduce anemia. Because of its chlorophyll content, it is an excellent mouthwash. Externally, a poultice made from wheat grass has been used by some people for cuts, sores, wounds, burns, boils, bee stings, and other insect bites.

I drink an ounce a day when it is available. It can be bought at most health food stores or you can easily grow your own.

Meat
Whenever Great Spirit gifts me with meat that has been hunted in an honorable way, I consider it a special gift from the cycle of

nature and part of the balance of life. I try to avoid all red meats from grocery stores but I'm not averse to red meat that has been hunted in a sacred manner. If the hunter honors the animal that has given its life and energy, it is good and I am grateful and will enjoy it. I begin all of my meals with a prayer of thanks to the Creator and to the Earth Mother. When the meat of an animal is part of the meal I make a special prayer of thanks. I honor the strength and courage of the animal and the rest of the species that lives on.

Venison steaks or rabbit stew are a sacred, delicious, and nutritious food source. If I am in a situation where I must eat meat, they are my first choices.

I have also been known to skin out a roadkill animal if it is still fresh and not badly damaged. I consider this holy, deep-energy food. But be sure it hasn't been in the sun for long.

If you live in a city and your only source for foods is a grocery store, buy chemical-free meat whenever possible and make special prayers for additional purification of your food. Eat more chicken and fish than red meat. Try to substitute other proteins for meat at least some of the time.

Vitamins

Because of the condition of our planet, a lot of food does not have all the energy it should. Consequently, I work a lot with vitamins and minerals. The following is a list of vitamins that have been beneficial to Crysalis, Sentinel Bear, other friends, and me. The list is limited to those vitamins and minerals that have been highly effective for our personal use. It is not a comprehensive list. Consult with your physician for which of these vitamins will work best for you.

THE GOOD GUYS AND BAD GUYS

To get a better idea of how to design your own diet plan, you need to have a basic understanding of which foods will help or harm you. To make it easy to remember, I divide foods into the "Good Guys" and the "Bad Guys." The "Good Guys" help prevent health problems and lead to a long fulfilling life. The "Bad Guys" contribute to the disease process.

If you absolutely cannot eliminate all of the "Bad Guys," you should at least consume items from that list with moderation.

I eat a pretty clean diet most of the time. However, I do treat

Vitamin/Mineral	What it Helps	Natural Sources
Vitamin A	Good for mucous membranes, bones, helps avoid respiratory infections, benefits eyes (particularly night blindness) hair, teeth, skin, and gums	Broccoli, cantaloupe, yellow fruits and vegetables, carrots, collards, and sweet potato

B vitamins (Note: B vitamins should not be taken alone). When I need B vitamins I eat more of the foods listed below. If that isn't enough, I supplement them with a multiple B-vitamin tablet, or a mixture of all the B vitamins listed here.

Vitamin/Mineral	What it Helps	Natural Sources
Vitamin B_1 (Thiamine)	Good for cells, muscles, heart, nervous system, mental attitude, appetite and digestion	Green peas, almost all vegetables, millet, garbanzo beans, split peas, rice, whole wheat, and buckwheat
Vitamin B_2 (Riboflavin)	Good for skin, nails, vision, hair and eyes, helps heal sores in the mouth, a good energizer	Collards, pinto beans, green leafy vegetables, skim milk, okra, and raw mushrooms
Vitamin B_3 (Niacin)	Good for skin, digestion, and nervous system	Brown and wild rice, chicken and barley

(*Note:* Niacin can produce symptoms of being flushed.)

Vitamin/Mineral	What it Helps	Natural Sources
Vitamin B_6 (Pyrodoxine)	Helps alleviate anemia, nausea, muscle spasms, good diuretic, good for skin, protein and fat metabolism, and for premenstrual syndrome	Cabbage, wheat bran, brewer's yeast, cantaloupe, banana, and tuna
Vitamin B_{12}	Increases mental and emotional vitality, assists memory, concentration, overall balance, and the nervous system	Fish, tuna, clams, dairy and animal protein
Vitamin B_{15}	Energizer, lowers cholesterol levels, builds stamina, can relieve angina, good for the liver and the immune system	Rice, seeds and grains

Vitamin/Mineral	What it Helps	Natural Sources
Vitamin C	Helps heal wounds, sores and burns, repairs tissue, helps with constipation, infections, colds, cough, helps lower cholesterol levels, helps bring stress under control, helps prevent blood clots, counteracts many allergies	Kale, oranges, sweet potatoes, raw green pepper, citrus fruit, berries, tomatoes, cauliflower, potatoes, strawberries, brussel sprouts, and oatmeal
Calcium	Good for bones, teeth, skin, hypoglycemia and fatigue, counteracts the toxic effects of some antibiotics, helps heal wounds, combats infection, ulcers, blood disorders	Skim milk, cooked green beans, whole grains, bran, chicken, green vegetables, cooked legumes, oranges, and broccoli
Copper	Good for red blood cells and iron storage, combats anemia, is an energizer	Beans, almost all seafoods, shrimp, peas, grapes, and whole grains
Vitamin D	Good for teeth, bones	Fish, tuna, salmon, and dairy products
Vitamin E	Good for skin (helps retard aging), vitality, stamina, combats fatigue, prevents scarring, helps to avoid and to destroy blood clots	Oatmeal, whole grains, brown rice, wheat germ, broccoli, leafy greens including spinach
Folic acid	Helps avoid food poisoning and parasites, good for skin, pain, sores in mouth (like canker sores), and anemia	Rye, leafy vegetables, spinach, greens, broccoli, whole wheat, carrots, cantaloupe, pumpkin, and beans
Iron	Good for blood, avoids anemia, helps skin, and prevents fatigue	Oatmeal, jerusalem artichokes, clams, dried fruit, peaches, millet, oysters, leafy greens, collard greens, and animal flesh

Vitamin/Mineral	What it Helps	Natural Sources
Magnesium	Helps prevent calcium deposits, good for indigestion, low mental attitude, depression, kidney problems, kidney stones, and gallstones	Lemons, acorn squash, corn, seeds, apples, cucumber, grapefruit, and zucchini
Potassium	Can help control allergies, can reduce blood pressure, helps carry oxygen to brain, and helps elimination	Whole grains, rice, whole wheat, millet, seeds, and poultry
Zinc	Helps avoid prostate problems, decreases cholesterol, helps heal open cuts, sores, and wounds, good for mental sharpness	Split peas, brewer's yeast, skim milk, oysters, wheat germ, cooked garbanzos, pumpkin seeds, whole wheat bread, and animal flesh.

myself sometimes. For instance, my favorite ice cream can only be purchased at a store in L.A. So when I'm in L.A., I'll splurge with ice cream.

Crysalis, however, rarely indulges in any of the "Bad Guys." Her idea of splurging is an all banana frugen from a health food eatery.

Moderation is a good rule of thumb, if you can make it work for you. If you do decide to splurge, set your limits and stick to them. If you are a compulsive person, and moderation has no earthly meaning to you, join a support group or twelve-step program like Overeaters Anonymous. The personal growth and freedom you receive will be much more fulfilling than any banana split.

If you are just beginning on a healthier path don't overwhelm yourself. Every two weeks drop another "Bad Guy" and add a new "Good Guy." Or begin by adding things from the "Good Guys," and drop the "Bad Guys" when you no longer want them. It will be sooner than you might think.

Keeping a food diary will help you set goals and honestly remember your food patterns. Without a diary, it is easy to forget if, when, and why you splurged with a "Bad Guy."

Good Guys	Bad Guys
Whole Grains	Caffeine
Complex carbohydrates	Salt
Fresh fruit	Sugars
Vegetables	Saccharin
Wheat Grass	Red meat
Fiber and roughage	Animal skins
	Fats
	Oils
	Alchohol
	Processed foods
	Preservatives
	Chemicals in food

Write your goals in your diet diary. Make a clear commitment on what date you will drop a "Bad Guy" or add a "Good Guy." Stick to it! You can do it! You're worth it! Reward yourself when you successfully fulfill a goal. Buy yourself something (not a food item) you've been wanting. Go to a movie. Get a massage or a manicure.

If you want to make a change in your diet, you'll need commitment, knowledge, and a good attitude.

TOOLS FOR CHANGE
Your nutritional formula should fit your needs, personality, and lifestyle. It may be necessary to change your way of perceiving taste but it shouldn't be necessary to compromise your total eating experience.

There are some excellent diets available today. The ones I use most are the Fit for Life diet plan and rejuvenation diets that revolve around raw fruits and vegetables, wheat grass, megavitamins, and supplements. Crysalis uses the Pritikin Program. Wabun uses a food group program similar to that recommended by the American Diabetes Association, except that she avoids dairy products.

You should consult with your physician before starting a new health program. Share your goals and ideas and ask for her support. Have her measure your cholesterol, triglycerides, and blood pressure. Keep a log of these. The recommended level for cholesterol is 100 plus your age. Triglyceride levels of 150 mg/dl are acceptable; however, 100 mg/dl is best. Also track your blood pressure: the optimum is 120/80. These three indicators can help you measure your improved health.

Here are some tools to help you begin to change your eating habits:

1. In your food diary identify the amounts, situations, and times when you overeat or go too long without food.
2. Acknowledge your motive for overeating or undereating. Were you overly tired? Stressed out? Lonesome? Angry?
3. Take the time to find an alternative activity to deal with those emotions interfering with healthy eating. If tired, then rest. If stressed, integrate stress release techniques. If lonesome, call a friend or support person. If angry, deal with the cause of your anger. By taking responsibility for your feelings and dealing with them, you also take back your power.
4. After you have determined your key problem eating times, plan a reward or alternative activity that will protect you from a binge. Just like the Boy Scouts, "Be prepared."
5. Remember food cravings only last about ten minutes. Be active in an alternative way until the craving passes.
6. Instead of excessive eating behavior, try exercise, or take a walk, listen to music, clean a closet, read the paper, make love, buy yourself something wonderful, play a musical instrument, meditate, get some bodywork done, or work in the yard. Try stretching, deep breathing, brushing your hair, brushing your teeth, smudging yourself, doing some form of ceremony, doing something playful with your mate or your children or pets, or give yourself a massage with oil.
7. Set limits and boundaries for when it is acceptable for you to splurge. Stick to these ground rules or get into a twelve-step program or support group immediately.
8. Eat regularly throughout the day. Make your meals smaller but consistent.
9. Keep acceptable snacks on hand.
10. Eat the best quality food you can find and afford at any given time. Organic produce tastes better and has more energy than chemically produced vegetables and fruits. The same is true of organic grains and meats. Buy them when you can.

11. Plan your menu for the week. Cook in advance. Prepare a big pot of soup, or cut up raw vegetables or fruit. Cook a pot of beans, rice, millet, or some other whole grain, then freeze it in portion sizes for future use. Bake potatoes and sweet potatoes at the same time. Wrap and refrigerate for later in the week.
12. Think in terms of permanent weight loss over a longer length of time. Losing four to six pounds a month equals fifty to seventy-two pounds a year. Not bad, Slim!
13. Remind yourself you are reducing the risk of heart disease, diabetes, cancer, hypertension, and other illnesses.

These techniques are the well-being weapons of a warrior. What may seem like a lot of work initially will become easy habits down the road.

As time goes on, you might experience some discomfort since your body needs to adjust to a different way of eating. Eating poorly can cause a toxic buildup in your system. As the toxins begin to clean out, you might experience cold symptoms, a change in bowel habits, fatigue, or skin eruptions. If any of these symptoms persist for more than a few days check with your health care practitioner.

OLD HABITS DIE HARD

After any initial discomfort, you should be rewarded with a lot of extra energy and a feeling of well-being. If you are underweight or overweight, as your weight approaches the normal range you will also feel better about how you look. Often, as you settle into your new eating pattern, even with its benefits, you'll be tempted by your old ways of eating. Like mind creatures, old habits die hard.

To help keep you focused on your nutrition plan at this critical time, try some of these recommendations:

1. Make a list of all the benefits of your healthy life style. Read it every morning and in your moments of weakness.
2. Set up a support system of family and friends who care and understand.
3. Don't miss support groups, twelve-step meetings, or therapy groups that you have designated as part of your health plan.

4. Talk with yourself. How long do you want to live? How much mobility do you want at an older age? Do you want to see your kids (grandkids) grow up? Do you want to stay sexual, vibrant, and frisky?
5. Learn from your slips and mistakes. Replace guilt with tools that resolve the real issues.
6. Keep in mind that obese people have a much higher disease and death rate. So do undernourished people, and those who binge and purge.
7. Listen to self-help tapes and videos.
8. Set goals. Reevaluate them at regular intervals.
9. Think of your diet as part of the game of life and enjoy playing.

When you successfully stick to your new health plan for a year, do something major for yourself. Go on a wonderful trip. Buy a new car. Get the piece of workout equipment you've always wanted. Go on a retreat, or to a seminar or workshop. Take a few days off and do nothing. Make it something really good. You deserve it.

Each year you stick to your rejuvenation program you will have added years on to your life. That is really good. You deserve lots of credit and a special reward. Plan your next healthy year and make it an annual event to reward yourself in a special way.

7 | Take a Walk

In the old ways, exercise was a natural part of life, integrated in all the activities of my people. Hunting, fishing, horseback riding, portaging canoes, and moving from camp to camp were all very physical activities that demanded stamina, strength, and energy.

When the Europeans first arrived in America, some of them referred to native Americans as the most physically well-developed and balanced human beings upon the face of the earth.

Native people took pride in themselves and in maintaining their bodies. The young children were always tremendous runners. In the time when there were forts all across the United States, one form of communication among them was the use of young Indian runners. They would travel 120–150 miles between forts with information and messages. This phenomenon was taken for granted. The native Americans were just considered incredibly fit and able. Compared to the Greek runners who would routinely run between cities and then die of exhaustion, they were in fact quite sensational.

Indian running takes particular skill and knowledge. The Tarahumara of Mexico are famed as runners. They have knowledge and special skills that allow them to run with speed and agility over long distances. In the local competitions in that area, it is commonplace to see these little, short Mexican Indians outrun tall, athletic Americans. The Tarahumara people call themselves "Raramuri" which translates as "runners on foot."

The Olympic runner, Jim Thorpe grew up on an impoverished reservation. Through intense self-belief and courage against many odds, he pushed on to become a champion runner, athlete, and

Olympic Gold Medal winner. At a time when the American Indians were a minority of about 300,000 people, he was chosen as the top all-American athlete. As a young man, he could easily have pigeon-holed himself, but he didn't. He fought against all odds, and trusted himself not to allow the negativity to stop him from reaching his goals and dreams. His story has always been an inspiration to me.

Exercise was so important in many cultures that it was integrated into the people's lives in sacred ways, often through dance. The sacred dances of the Hawaiian people, like the Hula, are, on one level, a form of exercise.

The same was true of the Maori people in New Zealand. They used dances on a physical plane to maintain good health through exercise.

The main emphasis in these dances was on the stomach and torso. The dances loosen up and strengthen this vital area that houses our most important organs. The Maoris felt this area was the sacred circle of the body, the focus of energy and life.

The Maoris believed one of the signs of a limber, unconstricted, physically fit body was the ability to move the bowels at least three times a day. They felt that you weren't walking your spiritual path in a sacred manner if you weren't healthy. Understanding this and working with exercise will help to bring you into balance and keep you going in a sacred way.

RUN AWAY EVERY DAY

Taking a walk is a wonderful experience. It is my favorite exercise. If you are feeling bad, angry, frustrated, or have low energy, walking can help you feel better. If you feel pressured, or can't relate to the people around you, or need an excellent, safe form of exercise, take a walk!

It is difficult to feel negative while your blood is pumping fresh oxygen through your body, and you see the beautiful Earth Mother all around you.

Whenever possible, walk in an area that is nice to view. Choose one that has wildlife like birds, rabbits, or squirrels. Be sure to wear comfortable clothing and shoes with good support. Do some stretches before you begin walking, then start out with a good brisk but enjoyable pace. Walk as long as you have to in order to change your mood, to get some good invigorating exercise, and to release any constricting emotions or anger.

Keep in mind that if you consciously "runaway" from home everyday by walking, you may avoid ever having to do so permanently. This is a positive form of "escape" that can give you perspective about life and a feeling that you can handle everything you need to do.

While you are out there, take time to talk with the wildlife, or hug a tree. Build your relationship with nature. Feel our Earth Mother's energy and let her life force fill and energize you.

Some time back, there was a popular TV commercial advertising batteries. The spokesman was a muscular fellow who had the physique of a wrestler. This man loudly and heftily proclaimed the batteries to be "The Energizer." His big line was "Gonna surprise ya, it's the energizer!" Well everytime you go for a walk anticipate this from our Earth Mother, because she might well surprise you. Think of her as the biggest battery pack ever. She is the real energizer.

Walking can be an excellent catalyst for a release of feelings, or a time for solving problems, making the big, seemingly insurmountable problems manageable. It's pretty hard not to mellow out a little when you are walking down a lovely path or a lane with nice trees, leaves floating to the ground, sun shining through the branches, and small critters prancing around you. Your perspective can't help but broaden. You'll get to where you can take a better look at what's really bothering you and deal with it in a healthier way. And if nothing is bothering you, walking is just a good way to spend part of your day.

There are many people who could avoid a lot of violence in their lives if they would just take the time for walking upon the earth, to acknowledge and really feel the life force beneath their feet.

Sometimes it feels good to take off your shoes and socks and walk barefoot. If you are in the city, or unfamiliar with the country, pick your spot carefully. Really feel the warmth, or coolness, and the firm support of the earth beneath you. Let it come into you, flow up into your being, and heal you. Let it balance you so that you are no longer carrying around negativity or anger. Allow yourself to become whole in a sacred manner.

Initially, feeling this earth energy may be a subtle experience, so give yourself time to slow down and really feel it. Eventually, it becomes so natural and easy to feel the powerful energy that the Earth Mother pours out, it will be hard to remember that the experience was ever subtle.

ENJOY YOUR EXERCISE

The best exercise program is one you truly enjoy, as I enjoy walking. It is important to look at what is available and choose a form of calisthenics you can look forward to. Don't try to be an Olympian the first week. Work up to your potential slowly.

Some great ways to exercise are walking, swimming, nature hiking, chopping wood, bicycling, walking on a treadmill, jogging, doing any of the martial arts, participating in Kamasutra sex, playing tennis, surfing, hoeing the garden, doing aerobic dancing, cranking up your stereo and dancing at home, rollerskating, weight-lifting, playing Zen golf or regular golf, doing interval and circuit training, hiking uphill, par courses, and rowing. We have all exercised at some time in our lives and we realize the benefits that are possible. Keeping some of these benefits in mind will help to encourage you to help yourself by keeping up with an exercise program.

Some of the benefits of exercise are increased strength, flexibility, energy, and sexual vitality as well as weight loss, better circulation, cardiovascular fitness, and improved digestion. Exercise will help eliminate poison and toxicity in the body. You may find you have healthier hair and nails, increased stamina, increased oxygen to the body, strengthened tendons, muscles, ligaments, and bones. Exercise will help you become more sensitive to your body. It can tone the body overall and help you look and feel younger. It is said to decrease osteoporosis and triglyceride levels. Exercise helps you have a better complexion. It encourages healthier eating, decreases stress, and increases depth of relaxation.

Initially, don't be concerned with the length of time you exercise. It is better to start off with fifteen minutes of enjoyable exercise than one hour of exercise you hate. As you build up your stamina, you'll naturally want to exercise for longer periods of time.

Eventually, you'll want to exercise three to five times a week for thirty-five to forty-five minutes at a brisk pace, stretching before and after your workout. But don't rush yourself. Be patient.

When you exercise should be determined by what is the most convenient and enjoyable time for you. It is a personal choice. Many people feel that exercise is a great way to start the day. Others like to work off the day's frustrations or tensions in the early evening. Decide by experimenting. Exercise at different times and see what works best for your body and schedule. Initially it will always seem difficult to fit exercise into your day. Do it anyway. Eventually you'll be happy you did.

STRETCH YOUR HEALTH

An important part of life and any exercise program is having good stretches all through your day, especially just before and after you work out. Stretching is beneficial for the muscles, joints, and oxygen flow. It assists your well-being by reducing tension, promoting circulation, breaking up energy blocks, and preventing injury. It also assists in developing and sustaining coordination. Stretching puts you in touch with a personal awareness and with the motion of your body. Best of all, stretching feels good!

Stretching is a part of all living creation, for all earth's children. Think of a dog or a cat when first they awaken from one of their many naps. Almost always they give themselves a nice long delicious stretch before they make their next move. In the wilderness, mountain lions, foxes, or coyotes all stretch when they awaken, unless they are in danger and must make a quick departure from their place of rest. Watch the trees or grasses stretch and bend with the wind.

Each morning I take time to consciously and leisurely stretch all my limbs, enjoying the feel of my body creating space, circulation, and motion. I consider it a bit of a slow-moving, relaxing dance that acknowledges and appreciates the life forces and energy that courses through my being.

Stretching Hints

1. Stretch each morning before you begin your day.
2. Stretch slowly, feeling the energy spread through your body.
3. Don't bounce when you are stretching.
4. Hold each position for twenty to thirty seconds. Keep in touch

with your body. Feel your feet planted firmly on the ground and feel the earth energy flowing up through you.

5. If a stretch is painful, ease up. Never push pain.
6. Breathe slowly, deeply, and regularly, allowing fresh air to permeate your being.
7. Begin and end every workout with a stretching routine.
8. Take time to stretch throughout the day.

Tips for Your Exercise Program

1. After stretching, take time to build your pace gradually in your workout. For the first five to ten minutes, exercise at a slow even pace. This allows your heart rate to increase safely and lets the blood vessels expand to assist the enlarged blood flow. Slow down at the end of your work out as well so that you can assist the reverse.
2. Remember, it's better to exercise for a shorter period of time, on a regular basis, than not to exercise at all. Just allow for a shorter stretch, warm up and cool down period.
3. Be positive about your workout. When negative thoughts come up, replace them with new positive ones. Create new habits and patterns in your life.
4. Don't eat immediately before or after you workout.
5. If you workout really hard one day, take it easy the next day.
6. If a muscle feels cramped or tense, stop and walk the tenseness out or stretch the muscle to avoid possible injury or cramp.
7. Keep your exercise equipment and workout clothes ready so when you get ready to exercise you are prepared.
8. Do not consume alcoholic beverages before you workout.
9. In hot weather, cut back on the pace and length of your workout. Drink lots of liquids. Allow your body to adjust to the heat of warm weather over a period of days. Wear sunblock.
10. Give your body time to cool down before jumping into hot or cold water. Radical temperature changes can place stress on your heart.
11. Don't skimp on shoes. Get the best support you can. Good shoes help avoid all-over injuries as well as injuries to the lower back, calfs, feet, or knees.

12. Stand in front of a mirror with no clothes on. Make an honest assessment of what changes you would like to make to your body. Visualize these changes. Acknowledge the wonderful parts of your body. Take time to admit what you really do like, and be honest about what you'd like to improve

13. Make your own list of benefits of your program. Keep this with you and in your food diary. When you are discouraged or think you're too tired to work out, read them.

14. Set realistic goals you will keep. When you reach them, set new goals. Achieve your goals one step at a time. Acknowledge your progress and when you accomplish a goal enjoy it.

15. Stay focused on your progress, not your failures.

16. Get whatever support or counseling necessary to clear out negative patterns that sabotage your efforts at having a positive body image and positive health habits.

17. Drink water. You can't drink too much water. Get an oversized glass and continue to fill it during the day. Make this a priority habit. Flush your system and avoid dehydration.

18. Allow your family and friends to support you.

19. Watch out for danger signs such as excessive fatigue, leg pains, chest, back, neck, and head pain or constriction, pain from an old injury, etc. If any of these occur, consult your physician.

20. Always consult a physician before beginning a new exercise program. Rarely will your doctor discourage you. However, there are some conditions you may not be aware of, or hidden symptoms that could result in a heart attack or other illness. It's always best to consult with a doctor initially, just to be sure.

21. If you have a pain or constriction in your head, chest, neck, or back, it could be angina. This comes from an inadequate supply of oxygen and blood to the heart. If you experience these symptoms stop exercising, and consult a physician.

22. If you experience extreme fatigue during your workout, especially in the legs, or dizziness or shortness of breath, you could be having a significant drop in your blood pressure. Stop your workout and consult a physician.

23. Leg pain, limping, or lameness can signal that clogged arteries are resulting in too small an amount of oxygen and blood being

received by the leg muscles, a condition called intermittent claudication. If you experience these symptoms, stop exercising and consult a physician.

24. There are exercise programs supervised by medical staffs in many hospitals and YMCAs. In these programs a trained nurse or doctor is available to monitor, assist, and consult with participants. If you have hypertension, a history of heart problems, claudication, back problems, or old injuries, you should consider such a program.

WATER OFF A DUCK'S BACK

A good walk usually gets me back on track when I'm feeling anxious or negative. I don't believe in letting worries or problems overwhelm me. Usually they just pass over me like water off a duck's back.

I've spent a lot of time working with the positive attitudes that allow me to stay calm. For those of you who are just beginning to bring your life to a more positive path, and for those of you who have times when you lose your cool, here are some tips to help you manage the stresses that are part of modern life.

1. Much of life is attitude. Maybe a lot of what bothers you doesn't really warrant the energy you expend on it. List your frustrations and evaluate them. See what you can put a big X through and drop from your list of personal torments.

2. Alleviate stress throughout your day by taking time to stretch, breathe, and listen to your body before you turn into a stress-pretzel.

3. Make time for yourself each day, and use it for whatever you really want to do.

4. Balance your life. Take time to relax as well as work.

5. Take more time to play with your dog or cat, children, mate, or friends.

6. Eat regularly throughout the day, stopping all other activities during your meals.

7. If you are dealing with a problem this month that you were dealing with three months ago, be responsible to yourself. Admit you need help. Turn to a therapist or a friend.

8. If you have a problem delegating work and responsibility, deal with it. Learn to share.
9. Dance can be a creative, relaxing, and stress-releasing process. Through free-form dance, you can express yourself and expand your ability to move and interact freely with a greater sense of awareness and vibrancy, while discharging stress.
10. Take time to enjoy your morning in some special way. Meditate, exercise, do ceremony, have a leisurely breakfast, or take an extralong bath.
11. Do you scream and yell in traffic? While some folks feel this behavior is okay, it can cause accidents. Discharge appropriately. Get in therapy. Usually the people who think they'll hate it the most love it. It's great to have permission to release all that pent-up emotion. Go for it, but in a way that is productive and brings about understanding and true release. Get rid of your stuff once and for all.
12. Learn and use some relaxation techniques like tai chi, yoga, zen meditation, transcendental meditation, guided imagery techniques, some ceremony, or being with the earth.
13. As you change your food and exercise habits, note that your stress level changes too. For most people, a healthier body reduces tension, making it easier for them to put their problems in perspective.

8 | Healing Herbs and Remedies

What happened to my people if they got sick? For thousands of years they didn't have aspirin they could take. But they did have willow bark, which contains salicylic acid, a natural substance that works similarly to aspirin. Native people considered nature to be their pharmacy. They knew about the medicinal uses of many plants, and of other natural substances.

Medicine men and women were so good at using the plants growing on this continent that early settlers affiliated with different denominations, and called medical evangelists, used to follow them around to learn their secrets. From this came the "folk medicine" used all across this country before medicine and pharmacology became the monopoly of certified doctors and druggists. A surprising amount of folk medicine has been incorporated into the medicine used today. Many of the old folk cures, in synthetic, chemical forms are widely used remedies now. For example, squaw tea (also called Mormon, Indian, and ephedra tea) was used by folk doctors to cure colds, congestion, and arthritis. The active ingredient in the tea is ephedrine. Pseudoephedrine is the main ingredient in many cold cures on the market now. Check for yourself at the local drugstore. Some medicine people used a carefully brewed tea made from foxglove to help folks with heart problems. The active ingredient in foxglove is digitalis. My grandmother used to use a particular mold if any of us got an infection. A similar mold forms the basis for penicillin.

Today, medical researchers have taken the place of medical evangelists in parts of the world where native people still use herbs for healing. For instance, researchers are studying the native plants in the Amazon, hoping to unlock the native people's healing secrets before their habitat is completely destroyed.

A Canadian herbalist friend of mine used to say she could cure almost anything using the twelve most common herbs growing around whatever area she was in. I believe she could. She had strong plant medicine. Many of you could also learn to deal with minor problems if you really knew the properties of the twelve most common herbs growing near your home.

I think the herbs growing near you are the best for you *if* (and this is an important if) you live in the country and in a relatively unpolluted area, and know the area well enough that you would recognize any new pollutants that had been introduced there. If you don't live in such a situation, but do desire to use herbs, the best kind to buy are those that are woodcrafted (or wild-crafted). Woodcrafted herbs are hand picked in an unpolluted area and are dried in the proper manner without the use of any chemicals. Then they are either packaged or made into capsules or tinctures. I have some apprentices and friends who have companies that provide woodcrafted herbs.

You need to be careful if you buy commercial herbs. Sometimes they are fumigated and irradiated as they are shipped from one country to another. Also, sometimes they are kept in storage for long periods of time. Ideally, an herb is used only in the first year after it is picked. It loses potency if it stays around longer.

If you want to try herbs for healing purposes, you can take them as teas, in capsules, or as tinctures. I like to drink herb tea and I know how to brew it properly, so that's a good way for me to use my plant brothers and sisters. Generally, to make a medicinal tea of leaves or flowers you use one tablespoon of herb to one cup of boiling water. You add the herb to the boiling water and let it steep about ten minutes before straining and then drinking. For roots, barks, and branches you use the same amounts but let them boil five minutes and then steep for five more. The amount of herb to water varies so be sure to check the proportions with an herbalist or a good herbal book.

Some folks either don't remember or don't want to be bothered with making and drinking enough cups of tea. Capsules or tinctures would work better for them. If you take encapsulated herbs, be sure to follow them with a cup of hot water so it can activate the herb. Tinctures also work better if you take them with warm water. If you don't like the taste of an herb you are better off sticking with capsules. If you want the herb to stay fresh longer, use tinctures, which have a longer shelf life than any other form of herb.

If you want to pick your own herbs, learn how to do it right from someone who knows what she is doing. A lot of herbs look alike at some stages of growth but might have very different effects. Picking the wrong herb could be deadly.

The world has changed a lot since the days when my people could go out and pick the herb they needed and use it without further concerns. They didn't have to contend with pesticides, or carbon monoxide fumes, or acid rain—all of which can turn a helpful herb into a poisonous one. I still encourage my students to pick herbs carefully, after they've learned how to do so, with respect and caution. A plant you pray over yourself before picking will have much stronger medicine for you.

Because many illnesses today are caused by chemical and other man-made changes in the environment, herbs and other natural remedies are not going to be the proper treatment for all illnesses or for all people. However, they can cure many problems if used with proper respect and guidance, and they can provide good strengthening if taken in addition to allopathic medications. Herbs are strong medicines in their own right, so be sure they enhance any other medications, rather than cause an adverse drug reaction.

Always respect herbs, and use them with care. Give them your love and prayers and they will help give you health.

Following is a list of common herbs with their most popular folk uses. If you are dealing with a persistent or serious problem, check with your health care practitioner before using an herbal cure.

Folk Herbs

Alfalfa. Aids stomach problems, arthritis, sinus troubles, hayfever, and the pituitary gland. It contains chlorophyll, which detoxifies the body, has high nutritional value, and stops internal bleeding.

Allspice. Helps toothaches when applied on the aching tooth. It also soothes the stomach and intestines, is energizing to humans, and soothing to nervous tummies.

Aloe Plant. Used for burns, scrapes, sunburn, insect bites, scratches, acne, sores, or itching. To use, open a section of an aloe plant leaf then rub the gel over the affected area. For burns, repeat every couple of hours on the first day. Then repeat four times a day until healed. It is important that burns are kept clean to avoid serious scarring or infection. For most other skin problems apply four times a day. My people and I use this with good results.

Amaranth. Helps with diarrhea, dysentery, and external wounds.

Angelica. Used for colds, intestinal problems, circulation, heart and lung troubles, viruses, flus, and stomach upset.

Anise Seed. Helps the pancreas, digestion, head colds, and dry coughs.

Basil. Aids the kidney, bladder, headaches, constipation, flus, colds, cramps, and fevers.

Bay Leaves. Good for indigestion.

Bayberry Bark. A laxative, it also helps the ovaries.

Bear Tribe Herbal Tobacco. A mixture of herbs we call *kinnikin-nik*. It is an alternative for people who want to quit smoking, and it has none of the poisons of tobacco.

Bee Pollen. A high energy food, is also good for allergies.

Birch Trees. These are among the most ancient and abundant trees. The bark and leaves can be used for teas and medicinal remedies. The vapor from leaves placed on hot rocks in sweat baths can help to cleanse the body of any problems it might have and also helps to rid it of static electricity. Branches of the birch can be bound together and used during sweats to thrash the body and help expel any toxins. Birch is good, when used as a tea, for skin conditions, arthritis, rheumatism, kidney problems, bladder and digestive problems, and to expel toxins. Birch encourages knowledge of ancient traditions and lost wisdom, and opens up energies that flow well. This is a Medicine Wheel herb.

Blackberry Leaves. One of the best herbs to stop diarrhea.

Black Cohosh. Good for female problems, and for strengthening and healing the lungs.

Black Pepper. A remedy for colds, sore throats, and sinus problems. A pinch of ground black pepper mixed with honey and taken everyday, is said to be a good preventative.

Black Spruce. Tips can be used as a tea or can be nibbled. High in vitamin C, it is good for an antiseptic and helps to loosen mucus in the throat and chest. The gum can be applied to cuts and wounds to clean them. It can be made into a plaster for setting bones and used on the face to protect it from sunburn. A tea from twigs makes a good bath and cures colds. The gum can also be used as an inhalant, both in and out of the sweatlodge. This is a Medicine Wheel herb.

Blue Camus. A good food staple. This plant can be used as a molasses or sugar substitute, and gives a food that has sustained people for thousands of years. It is good for balancing blood sugar levels and, in the proper quantities, as a purgative and emetic. This plant is excellent for creating movement where there is stagnation. It is very important to use only blue colored camus. Any camus with yellow or greenish-white flowers can make you very sick or worse. This is a Medicine Wheel herb.

Blue Cohosh. Helps cramps.

Blue Flag. Helps cure constipation.

Boneset. Helps fevers, flus, and digestion.

Buchu. A diuretic good for kidney, urethra, and bladder problems.

Burdock. A blood purifier, and diuretic, it is also good for the ovaries.

Calmus. Helps the liver, stomach, and intestines.

Caraway. Good for gas and indigestion.

Cardamom. Helpful for diarrhea, gas, and indigestion. It has a warming influence on the body.

Catnip. Helps headache and soothes the stomach and nerves. Good for colicky babies.

Cayenne Pepper. Dilates constricted blood vessels and helps to cure colds.

Chamomile. A calmant and sedative, it is good for digestion, stomach, insomnia, kidneys, bladder, liver, toothaches, headache, and the nervous system.

Chaparral. Good for infections and inflammations of the urinary tract and intestinal tract. Also helps with colds, flus, parasites, and other bacterial infections.

Chickweed. A diuretic and laxative. It is used externally for open sores.

Chicory. A coffee substitute, it is good for the liver, eyes, skin, kidneys, stomach, and for hepatitis and alcoholism.

Cinnamon. A mental stimulant that encourages astuteness and clarity. It is good for coughs, cramps, diarrhea, stomachache, and heart pain.

Cleavers. A diuretic good for urinary obstructions.

Cloves. Help toothaches (applied on aching tooth) and intestines. They are energizing and soothing to nervous tummies.

Coltsfoot. An expectorant for lungs and bronchial areas. Aids indigestion.

Comfrey Leaves. A blood cleanser, soothes the stomach, stops internal bleeding, helps expel gallstones, aids headaches, cuts, and burns. They make a good external poultice.

Comfrey Root. A blood cleanser, it is good for ulcers, stomach, kidneys, bladder and bowels, coughs, and colds.

Coriander. A good diuretic and fever reducer.

Corn Silk. Helps cure urinary tract infections.

Cumin. Reduces gas and is a stimulant.

Dandelion. The root is good as a coffee substitute and herbal remedy. The greens make a good cooking herb. The young dandelion greens can be used in salads. They are high in vitamins A, B, C, and G, calcium, phosphorous, iron, and natural sodium that helps to purify and alkalize the bloodstream. Dandelion can be used for cleansing all of the eliminative organs of the body. It is soothing, considered a sedative, relaxing, and a diuretic. It is said to help balance the blood sugar levels in the body. Dandelion is a Medicine Wheel plant.

Echinacea. A blood purifier, heals ulcers, infections, insect bites, abcesses, sores, and wounds.

Elder. Flowers relieve constipation and reduce fever.

Ephedra. Relieves congestion and helps heal arthritis.

Eucalyptus. Stimulates circulation and is a good decongestant.

Fennel. Aids the liver, pancreas, digestion, and cramps.

Flax Seed. Good for urinary tract infections, kidney and bladder inflammations, and bowel problems.

Fenugreek. Helps cure infections, headcolds, liver and sinus problems. It is an energizer.

Garlic. The world-renowned home remedy. Good for hypertension, headaches, lung troubles, nervous disorders, and parasites.

Ginger. A digestive aid and an energizer, it reduces gas and constipation.

Ginseng. An energizer and aphrodisiac that also stimulates pituitary and thyroid activity and is good for coughs, colds, and digestion.

Goldenseal. Good antiseptic and tonic. It helps the bladder, colon, and mucous membranes. It is good for flu, skin eruptions, nose-bleeds, sore throats, stomach distress, and some infections.

Gotu Kola. Aids the energy level, helps relieve depression, promotes longevity, and helps the heart, memory, and brain.

Hops. A relaxant, sedative, and blood cleanser. They help cure headaches and insomnia, kill worms, and are useful in expelling poisons.

Horse-radish. A stimulant, decongestant, and blood purifier.

Horse-tail. A blood coagulator, diuretic, and good for urinary ailments.

Horehound. Helps cure congestion, coughs, lung and throat problems, and ulcers. It is a laxative and an antidote for poisons and venomous bites.

Jasmine. A sedative and aphrodisiac. It relieves indigestion.

Juniper Berries. Help indigestion, coughs, and skin diseases. They are a good diuretic.

Kelp. Helps the thyroid, arteries, and nails. It cleanses radiation from the body.

Lady-Slipper. Aids insomnia, hysteria, and headaches.

Lavender. Helps cure cramps.

Licorice Root. Good for hypoglycemia, adrenal gland problems, stress, and colds.

Lilac. Helps cure cramps.

Marjoram. Good for coughs and colds.

Mate. A good stimulant and purgative.

Mullein. Tea is good for soothing mucous membranes and for helping with lungs, heart, bladder, kidney, and liver problems. Mullein is conducive to alleviating nervous conditions and is a general astringent. Externally, the tea is good for hemorrhoids, ulcers, tumors, swelling of the throat, and muscle tenderness. Oil made from mullein flowers has long been used for eardrops, wart removal, and to relieve bruises, sprains, and chapped skin. Mullein is a Medicine Wheel plant.

Mustard Seed. A stimulant, diuretic, laxative, and blood purifier.

Nettle. Helps reduce anemia, exhaustion, backache, and poor circulation.

Nutmeg. Aids indigestion, nervous disorders, and heart problems. Pregnant women should not take nutmeg.

Orange Peel. Good for indigestion, colds, diarrhea and the reduction of mucus.

Oregon Grape Root. A tonic and blood purifier. It improves digestion.

Parsley. Helps with female problems, stomach, kidney, and bladder. Parsley is a great breath freshener and expectorant.

Pennyroyal. A sedative and pain reliever. It helps with scratches, sores, insect and snake bites, itching, cramps, and backache. (Note: pregnant women should avoid this herb.)

Peppermint. Helps cure gas, nausea, vomiting, diarrhea, coughs and colds, headaches, and grumpy colons.

Plantain. A healing plant which can be used both internally and externally as a tea or as a compress to cool, soothe, and heal. It has been known to be a good blood cleanser, and to alleviate pain. In some cases, plantain will reverse the effects of some poisons. Used as a tea, compress, or in a bath, it can help heal sores, stings, ulcers, inflammation, and kidney and bladder trouble. Plantain is a plant of the Medicine Wheel.

Poke Root. A blood purifier, it reduces bronchial inflammation.

Quaking Aspen. Leaves, bark, and buds can be used for a tonic or tea to aid in liver and digestive disturbances. It is also used as a relaxant, and for faintness, hay fever, and the internal organs. Quaking aspen has been used daily to help with skin conditions such as eczema, ulcers, and burns. The powder scraped from the bark can be used as a deodorant and has been said to help treat cataracts. Teas and tonics from the quaking aspen can help prevent congestion in the body, hay fever, asthma, bronchitis, and toxicity. Quaking Aspen is a plant of the Medicine Wheel.

Raspberry. Leaves, root, twigs, and berries are all medicinal. The berries are cleansing to the system. Raspberries can be used for breaking up and expelling gallstones and kidney stones. They stimulate action of the urinary organs. The root is an astringent and has some antibiotic and healing properties. It can be used as a gargle for sore throats. The tea as a compress has been applied successfully to wounds and cuts to stop bleeding. A tea from the leaves can be used for diarrhea, cankers, uterus problems, and for promoting healthy pregnancies and menstruation. A tea from the twigs is good for colds, flus, difficulty in breathing, and for balancing blood sugar levels. Raspberry is a Medicine Wheel plant.

Red Clover. A blood purifier and fever reducer. It is good for anemia.

Red Sage. An aphrodisiac, diuretic, and stimulant. It helps with female troubles, gas, anxiety, headaches, and liver problems. It is also good for coughs, colds, and for strengthening and healing lungs.

Rhubarb. Good for indigestion and diarrhea caused by irritation of the intestines.

Rose Hips. Help the adrenal glands, circulation, and give an energy boost. They are some of the richest natural sources of vitamin C.

Rosemary. Good for headaches, coughs, colds, gas, indigestion, and female problems.

Sage. Helps cure colds, flu, diarrhea, and bladder infections.

Sassafras. Purifies the blood and helps toothaches and skin problems.

Slippery Elm Bark. Aids in treating ulcers, grumpy stomach, bladder, moody bowels, inflamed mucous membranes, and general aches and ouchies.

Spearmint. Soothes the nerves and stomach.

Thistle. Good for stomach and digestive problems. It helps to reduce fever, expel worms, increase milk in nursing mothers, and strengthen internal organs. The young stem or root of the thistle can be peeled and eaten raw or cooked. The fruitlike seeds can be eaten raw or roasted. All parts of the thistle are rich in minerals. Thistle is a Medicine Wheel plant.

Thyme. Helps with cramps, headaches, diarrhea, coughs, and laryngitis. Thyme is a good appetite stimulant.

Turmeric. Aids in relief of cramps, congestion, fevers, and nosebleeds. It is a blood purifier and, applied externally, helps heal wounds.

Uva Ursi. A tonic and diuretic that is good for female problems and kidney and bladder troubles.

Valerian. A sedative, calmant and muscle relaxant. It soothes cramps, spasms, and hypertension. It is good for the bladder.

Violet. Encourages warm sentiments of the heart. Both the leaves and the flowers are good as an antiseptic and as an expectorant. It can be used as a thickener in stews and as a flavoring in hot dishes, salads, jams, and syrups. Medicinally, it is good for penetrating the blood and lymphatic fluids and dissolving toxins in those areas. Violet assists in the healing of cancer, toxicity in stomach or bowels, sore throats, difficulty in breathing, or tumors of the throat. It helps cool high temperatures, and may alleviate ear problems and headaches. Used as a compress, it is good for headaches, toothaches, sore throats, and skin problems. Violet is a plant of the Medicine Wheel.

White Oak. Used as a poultice on skin irritations, wounds, and snake and insect bites. Good for gums and infections of the vagina, and for uterine problems.

Wild Rose. Hips are high in vitamin C and are excellent for sore throats, colds, and flus. You can use the plant as a tea, tonic, or bath, all with effective results. Rose tea is good for an astringent and effective in treating gallstones, kidney stones, bladder, or liver problems. Rose is refreshing to the spirit and good for any problems requiring a gentle cooling effect. Rose water is good for eye lotions and helps alleviate the discomfort of hay fever. Wild rose is a Medicine Wheel plant.

Witch Hazel. Good used externally on bites, burns, hemorrhoids, and wounds.

Yarrow. Terrific as a tonic and strengthener. Yarrow has been used with good results for the digestive tract and as a blood cleanser. It relieves colds, flus, and other related diseases. It acts as a diuretic if you need one. It helps to open pores to allow the skin to eliminate toxins. Yarrow also soothes the mucous membranes. This plant can be used during pregnancy and at birth to prevent hemorrhage. Externally, yarrow acts as a local anesthetic and disinfectant. To relieve mosquito-bite itch, chew the leaf, then put it on the mosquito bite. To relieve toothache, chew the leaf and let the juice flow over the painful tooth. Yarrow is also said to be good for the lungs, glands, and bronchial tubes. Yarrow is a Medicine Wheel plant.

Yellow Dock. An aide for rheumatism and skin eruptions. It is a blood purifier and laxative. Good for liver and stomach.

Yerba Santa. Helps cure congestion and asthma and can be used externally for poison oak.

HOME REMEDIES

I have found that herbs often work better for me in combination than when taken alone. I have some favorite combinations, and so do Crysalis, Peter, and Wabun. Here, we'd like to share with you some of the cures that we've actually used for colds, flus, minor infections, and assorted complaints with good results. We don't promise that these cures will benefit you in any way, but they have helped us. If you are pregnant, dealing with a small child, or seriously or persistently ill, you should, of course, see a doctor.

Aches and Pains

If you have aches or pains try this mixture of two tablespoons of equal parts of valerian, catnip, peppermint, skullcap, mint, cloves, nettle, and mullein brewed in four cups of water. Drink hot or cold, two to four cups.

Bladder Problems

Cook eight cups of fresh water with four tablespoons of a tea consisting of equal parts of chamomile, juniper berries, comfrey, sassafras, slippery elm, goldenseal, spearmint, uva ursi, and valerian for ten minutes. Steep for another five minutes. Drink three cups daily for five to seven days. Save the tea and reheat it, or drink it cold.

Colds and Flus

The cold is one common sickness that can respond well to home remedies. So can some simple flus. If you are getting the sniffles, take one gram of vitamin C (preferably organic) four to ten times a day. That may do the trick. If not, try *chewing* (don't just swallow) one large clove of organic garlic in the morning, and one at night. Chew some parsley afterward to get rid of the taste. If you still can't stand the taste, try cutting a small garlic clove into tiny pieces, putting it in a cup, and mashing it. Add the juice of one-quarter of a small lemon. Brew a cup of herb tea—mint is good—and add the garlic and some honey. Let it sit for three minutes. Drink a cup three times a day until the cold is gone. This has been known to cure bad colds, that have gone to the throat or ears, in four days. My favorite cold/flu remedy is hot apple cider vinegar and honey tea, which is made by adding a cup of boiling water to two to three tablespoons of vinegar and as much honey as you need to make it drinkable. Less courageous folks substitute lemon juice for vinegar in this recipe.

An herbal cure we've used for colds, flus, and other infections caught in the early stages is our herbal infection mixture. It consists of one part goldenseal powder to two parts each of myrrh and echinacea powder. This really tastes bad, so we put it in capsules and take three or four of them each day.

If you can rest as soon as you feel a cold or flu coming on, that helps a lot. So does a long, tepid, soaking bath. Also, be conscious not to expose other people to your mucus.

Teas we've found that help to cure colds and flu are yarrow, comfrey leaf, and chamomile mixed together. Usually we put a tablespoon of each in about a quart of boiling water, and let it steep for twenty minutes. If this is all you'll be using for a home cure, make it medicine strength, which is one tablespoon of the mixture to one cup of water. We also have used ephedra (squaw) tea to relieve nasal congestion.

The Mother Mulligan method for curing colds and flus consists of making a tea using peppermint, ginseng, nettle, rosemary, saffron, valerian, goldenseal, pennyroyal, yarrow, sage, and pleurisy root. Turn off your phone, turn on soft music, curl up with a good book, a warm blanky, a teddybear, and drink lots of this tea. When hungry, eat light—toast and preferably home-cooked soup. You'll feel better in no time at all. And don't forget, wear your slippers and warm socks when you are up padding around the house. (Note: Pregnant women should leave out the pennyroyal.)

A good tea for coughs is one we make using equal parts of coltsfoot, ginseng, marjoram, rosemary, red sage, comfrey, and two parts of peppermint. Drink it hot.

Colon Troubles

For Grandma Coyote's grumpy colon remedy, simmer two tablespoons of equal portions of bayberry bark, goldenseal, and peppermint in four cups of water. Cook for fifteen minutes, let steep for five minutes more. Drink two cups a day for two days. Repeat if necessary.

Cramps

Brew a strong mixture (two tablespoons of herbs in two cups of water) of equal parts blue cohosh, thyme, pennyroyal, and fennel. Drink it hot. Then take a hot bath with a mixture of one-quarter cup of lavender or lilac flowers dried or fresh, one-quarter cup of rose petals, and one-half cup of sesame oil. Put a cool rag over your forehead. If it is still necessary, place a heating pad over the painful area. If serious cramps are a monthly occurence rest whenever possible during the first day or two of your moon time. (Note: Pregnant women should not use pennyroyal.)

An alternative mixture for cramps and other female problems is to simmer in six cups of water three tablespoons of an equal mixture of dandelion root, rosemary, slippery elm, black cohosh, parsley, and red sage for twenty minutes. Drink one to three cups daily. Save the remains and reheat when needed. (See Ovarian Problems.)

Fever

If we have a fever, sometimes we take large capsules filled with cayenne pepper (capsicum). The cayenne helps us to sweat more profusely, ridding our bodies of the toxins so that the fever can break. Also, we sometimes take a cayenne capsule followed by some lemon juice before we take our sweats, as this causes us to sweat more and get rid of more toxic matter. Cayenne speeds up your heart and circulation, so be cautious if you have any heart problems. Some tribal medicine people use sweats to make a fever run its course more quickly. We don't recommend that a lay person use this method. Instead, use cold baths or alcohol rubs given every fifteen to thirty minutes until the fever is down, or sponge the person off with cool cloths. In between coolings, be sure the person is covered well so that they don't chill.

For teas to combat a fever, take peppermint, elder flower, and yarrow tea. Drink, then go to bed. The tea works by opening up the pores so that the toxins can come out. This has been reported to be okay for children. Medicine-strength sage tea is also good. If the fever is 104 degrees fahrenheit or higher, it is *dangerous*, and you'd better get to a doctor fast.

For stomach flu (or poisoning) the quickest cure we've found is taking large capsules of goldenseal powder along with vitamin C. We've taken them every hour or two, for up to eight hours, and been rid of all the flu symptoms. When we have stomach flu, we don't try to eat until we feel like it, and usually we start off with citrus fruit. Peppermint, chamomile, and comfrey tea, separately or together, seem to settle the stomach. You can also try vinegar and honey tea for stomach flu.

Headaches

Brew a strong mixture of catnip, peppermint, chamomile, rosemary, and thyme. Take time to sit back and stretch out, with your feet elevated on a foot stool (not above hip level) and drink this tea while it is hot. Drink the tea slowly. Take long deep breaths in between large sips of tea. Continue to sit comfortably for at least fifteen minutes, concentrating only on a long slow deep breathing process. If you are sleepy, allow yourself at least a short nap.

Running water, as hot as you can stand without scalding yourself, over your wrist or taking a very hot bath or shower will open up the capillaries to the head and help to relieve headaches.

Processed foods, caffeine, perservatives, salt, high-sugar foods, chemicals, and drugs are all items that separately or together can cause painful headaches and migraines. If you have a chronic headache problem, take an honest look at your intake of any or all of the above items.

Kidneys

Brew a large batch of this tea and drink it daily for two to three weeks for a really thorough kidney flush. You can drink it hot or cold. The tea is made with one tablespoon of herb mixture to two cups of water. The herb mixture is equal parts of cayenne, birch, comfrey, goldenseal, spearmint, uva ursi (this grows wild at Vision Mountain and in many heavily forested areas), juniper berries, chamomile, bitterroot, beech, black cohosh, parsley, sage, and dandelion. Sentinel Bear recommends this mixture highly.

Laxative

Castor oil is an old remedy that hasn't become any more pleasant with age but is still very effective. When you take it, be ready for the results. At the Bear Tribe, anyone who uses castor oil sticks close to the outhouse and most likely has a magazine or good book with them. I say, "Always make the most of each situation." A good herbal remedy for constipation is an equal parts mixture of sage, goldenseal, and mullein. This can be brewed as a tea or taken in capsule form. Cassara sagrada is also very effective. So is an enema. If you eat enought fiber, or take psyllium husks to add fiber to your diet, you should rarely have problems with constipation.

Liver Flush

The liver is the primary detoxifier of the body. In today's world, it can often be overburdened. This happens due to overzealous drinking of alcoholic beverages, eating processed foods or too much grease, taking drugs and chemicals, caffeine, or other pollutants. When you feel that you have overextended your liver, you can try this liver flush. Squeeze two lemons, keeping the pulp, seeds and juice, add two cloves of garlic cut into slices, four to five ounces of fresh water, and one tablespoon of cold-pressed olive oil. Add two fresh oranges or a fruit of your choice for flavor. Blend these ingredients and drink it first thing in the morning. Wait about twenty minutes, then drink a glass of hot water. Eat lightly on the days you are doing this liver flush and drink a lot of hot herb tea.

Nervousness

To calm down, brew two cups of water with two tablespoons of equal parts of peppermint, chamomile, passion flower, rosemary, thyme, valerian, spearmint, and blue violet. Simmer for twenty minutes. Drink slowly while it is still relatively hot. After drinking the tea, sit comfortably or lie down, for at least ten minutes. Do long, very slow, deep breathing. Repeat this twice daily or as needed.

Ovarian Problems

Brew a large pot of tea, using equal parts of black cohosh, blue cohosh, bayberry bark, burdock, and pennyroyal (one tablespoonful of herbs to one cup of water). Drink two cups a day for one month, and as much as three cups daily during your moon time. For ten minutes a day for one month sit or lie comfortably with a heating pad across your lower abdomen covering your ovaries during your moon time. This remedy has helped to heal some chronic ovarian problems. If problems persist, notify your physician. This can be used in addition to other remedies or suggestions from your physician. (Note: Pregnant women should not use pennyroyal.) (See Cramps).

Sinus Problems
Brew two cups of water with two tablespoons of a mixture of equal parts of bayberry, eucalyptus, sage, and goldenseal. To help open your sinuses, you can place a towel over your head like a little tent and lean over the simmering pot, breathing deeply, inhaling the steam, for five to twenty minutes. After this mixture brews for twenty minutes, drink it relatively hot.

9 | Spiritual and Ceremonial Healing

Much of the sacred information about different spiritual and ceremonial avenues of healing and growth has been with us for centuries. With the earth changes that are coming about, I strongly feel that now is the time to bring back and share many of the old ways. These old teachings and ceremonies can help guide people on their path, as well as promote better health.

This world is a place for you to grow and learn to know your power and your spirituality. This is your responsibility. In my journeys I see people opening up more rapidly to their universe. They are sifting through the layers and seeing what is real and what isn't in shorter periods of time. These happenings are essential at this time because we are moving into a period of major earth changes and other powerful events. Spirit says that there will be a strong core of people who will be teachers and guides for others during this transition time.

It is right to share tools and knowledge that can help our family of human beings walk the sacred path, a path that teaches love and respect for ourselves and our Earth Mother. This is why I am doing the work I am doing right now. This is why I spend so much time teaching my apprentices, doing workshops, and bringing large groups together at Medicine Wheel Gatherings.

MAKING MEDICINE

Medicine takes many different levels and forms. In the native American path we make medicine for everything, for a good hunt, for the crops to be bountiful, for a birthing to go well, for connecting with a loved one, for healing someone, for a situation to go a certain way, for winning a game or sport, etc. Making medicine is an important and integral part of our lives. When someone comes to me for help or healing, and asks me to do a pipe ceremony for him, he is asking me to make medicine. Medicine is our way. It is how we give gratitude and thanks to the spirit that moves in all things, and to the spiritkeepers who help us, guide us, nourish, and clothe us. Medicine is a constant pipeline to the Creator and the means by which we keep our balance with the circle of life that sustains and maintains us, consistently giving us the opportunity to reenvision life in a new and more healthy way.

The native American way is to "feel" these powers and forces we work with. They are as real to us as the ground beneath you is to you. We have connections and ways through our medicine and medicine objects to communicate with the powers of life, with spirit. And if you call to Spirit, Spirit will always answer.

Medicine Objects
The items we use to help us make medicine are called medicine objects. Medicine objects can be anything that relates to the Creator in a sacred way.

If you need to keep a variety of medicine objects with you, use a medicine pouch or medicine bag. A medicine bag is a pouch (usually small) in which medicine objects and sacred articles are carried and kept close to their keeper. Often it is worn like a necklace, hanging around the neck or over the heart. These bags may have many different items in them, everything from herbs for healing to a crystal, or a gift someone has given you to a claw from one's animal totem. Your medicine objects are all personal and worked with in a sacred manner.

Native Americans are very protective of their medicine pouches and bags. These bags carry a part of themselves, or of others, that is powerful and sacred. Sometimes people reach out to touch my medicine pouch. Many medicine people don't care for this touching because it blends this new person's energy with the energy of the medicine pouch or object. Personally, it is not a problem for me. After someone touches the medicine object, I put my hands over it and recharge it with my own energy. This is called taking power over something. I prefer it if people ask before touching something however.

Power Gifts

People come to me and give me medicine objects as a medicine pledge. This is a pledge of their support for me and of my support for them. If they need help or I need help, I can pray and hold that object and their power comes through to support me, or I send them my love, strength, or healing. If I have some very heavy work to do, they'll send me their power to back me up.

I have a pouch that contains four gold coins. These are medicine coins that were given to me in California by a Bronco Apache. The Bronco Apache are a people who say they have never eaten the bread of the white man. They live as they always have, south of Tucson, moving back and forth across the border between Mexico and the United States without asking anyone's permission, and doing very much as they please. Both governments ignore them as long as they don't go on the warpath.

These extremely valuable coins are part of a collection that dates from the time when stagecoaches would come through Apache Pass and the Apaches would liberate the stagecoaches of their cash boxes. These coins have been in the Apache families for many, many years. When my friends need a little extra money for hunting equipment, or some flour or beans, they might take a few of these coins to a special rare coin dealer whom they trust. These four coins were given to me by my friend, so I cherish and treasure them. He said he gave them to me because I was the only Indian he knew who was really doing anything for the Indian people in a substantial way. This was back in Los Angeles when I was working with many native Americans in many different ways. So I carry them with honor and feel happy this gift has been given to me. Different gifts like this are power gifts. Another power gift I have is a crescent half-moon necklace with coins dangling from it that a gypsy chief gave me as a pledge of his support. He also was a medicine man and this medicine object carries some of his powers. When I pray with it, I can ask for help and it will help me. When I give a medicine gift, the same holds true. The person I give the gift to can hold it and pray and my energy goes through it to him. Knowing this is all a part of understanding medicine.

As you go along the medicine path, you may be given gifts.

Understanding how to deal with them and respect them is crucial. Many gifts can come directly from Spirit through nature in the form of a rock, feathers, or an animal bone found while walking in the woods or anyplace on the earth.

All gifts that come to you should be smudged and prayed over, and you should give thanks and ask for guidance on how best to use the gift. Some gifts you may not be ready to receive. One time, I was doing a workshop in Sedona, Arizona with Page Bryant and a woman gave me a little piece of a pyramid. Shortly after, I began to feel really sick, with a lot of pain, particularly in the area behind the pocket where I had the little piece of pyramid. Upon realizing this, I removed the gift and set it on the ground next to me. The pain and illness disappeared. Later that night, when I was alone in my room, I decided to experiment with it. Sure enough, if I placed it in my pocket I began to feel very sick, but when I removed it and set it away from my body I was just fine. I concluded that I wasn't ready to handle this yet. I needed to watch and pray over it. This empowered medicine object needed to tell me how to use it or if I was supposed to give it to someone else who is ready to work with this type of ancient energy. It is important always to pray over newly acquired medicine objects and learn about them before beginning to use and work with them.

I have a medicine stick with a carved face on it and corn on the side. When it was given to me, I knew it was powerful and that I had to work with it very carefully. So I brought it home and prayed over it and did ceremony, asking for the spirit that belonged to it to come into it. I prayed to know how best to use it and thanked the spirits for giving me this powerful medicine. The more I prayed with it and did ceremony the more I understood what could be done in terms of working with it.

Well, some time went by, then one day, during an apprentice program, the medicine stick let it be known that it wanted to join me that day, so I brought it with me. The group of apprentices I was working with were a bit slow to grasp some of what I was trying to share about medicine and the power of nature, and were just taking some of the things in the program and life in general for granted. I said, "Hmm, okay. Let's go up to the top of the hill and make a circle by the teepee." When everyone was situated, I began praying with the stick and the energy started picking up.

Although it had been a very still and calm day, the winds picked up. In a matter of moments, the wind was blowing so hard that the teepee was almost knocked over. Pages from the apprentices' notebooks were flying around amidst people's hats that had blown off the tops of their heads. Everyone was holding on to their belongings for all they were worth. After acknowledging all this I said, "Ho, Great Spirit!" Immediately, all was perfectly calm and still. Needless to say we had the apprentices' complete attention for the rest of that program. That stick proved to be a very powerful medicine object.

CEREMONIAL HEALING

At the Bear Tribe, we conduct many ceremonies that encourage cleansing and healing of ourselves and reconnection with our Earth Mother, such as the Sweatlodge Ceremony (also called the Stone People's Lodge), the Pipe Ceremony, Smudging, the Medicine Wheel Ceremony, the Vision Quest, Full Moon Ceremonies, as well as other ceremonies. If the native path appeals to you, some of these ceremonies might become a part of your healthy lifestyle. I'll describe the ceremonies a little here. To really learn about them you'll need to participate with properly trained people who conduct them. Some of these people are listed in Appendix A.

Smudging

Smudging is a powerful ceremony for cleansing and purifying your energy field through the use of smoke from burning herbs. To smudge you light special herbs then draw the smoke over your body. The smoke clears negativity, and cleanses, focuses, and purifies the energy field of the person smudging, or the place that is smudged. In the Bear Tribe, we draw the smoke over our heads, to our hearts, over each shoulder, and down the arms then down the body. Usually we use sage, sweetgrass, and maybe cedar, although smudge is not limited to these herbs. Crysalis has a favorite mixture that is a blend of sage, rose petals, lilac, and lavender. Most of the herbs connected with the Medicine Wheel as plant totems can be burned as smudge and will draw in the energy and qualities of the corresponding totem.

Sometimes I use copal (pine resin) on charcoal, especially to smudge a powerful mask I work with. A Mayan spiritual brother has been teaching me about the powers and usage of the mask, so I use traditional Mayan smudge. This large wooden, beautifully carved mask made me a sort of conductor for the wisdom and other deep teachings, guidance, and knowledge of the Mayan people. One night, I had my first dream guided by this mask. I had placed the mask over my head earlier in the evening and lay with it and worked with it and it's energies before I went to sleep. Because of this, I had a very powerful experience through my dream state. In the dream, I was going through the jungle of South America. At different sacred spots, I was smudged with the copal. As the smudging took place, I found ancient relics of those olden cities, such as knives and different offerings, that had been made by the elder people. This and three other dreams I had were very powerful. I am grateful for this. I prayed for these dreams and my prayers were answered. To show respect for this honor, I led a special smudging ceremony to honor Spirit and the mask that was the channel for spirit guidance.

Smudging is a universal practice known to religions throughout the world. In Catholic churches they use frankincense; in Buddhist temples, sticks of incense. Before any ceremony, we smudge ourselves and all sacred objects that are used so we can be centered and focused for whatever follows.

Drumming and Chanting

Drumming and chanting are powerful ways to bring your energy into harmony with the energy of the earth, the sky, and the elements as well as the energy of other people. When you chant, it is good to know the words and the tune correctly, out of respect for the chant. Try to allow the music of the chant to come from your whole body, not just from your throat. Chanting is a form of prayer through music. The more you put into it, the more the power builds.

Drumming is a way to bring yourself into harmony with the heartbeat of the Earth Mother. It is also a way to take your mind out of everyday realities and into spheres where you can learn many new things. When I used to travel to powwows I loved going to sleep to the drumming of the stick game drums. That beat would stay in my mind for many days afterward. Once you hear the beat of the hand drums, or of the big dance drums, it is likely you won't ever forget it.

Many of the native people I've worked with use drumming or rattling, as well as chanting, as part of the means to bring about healing. There are certain sounds and rhythms that can help to bring you into harmony with different aspects of the Creation. Learning to chant and drum can help you find these sounds and rhythms.

The Pipe Ceremony

The pipe represents the universe to native American people. The pipe is an altar that we take with us wherever we go. The bowl represents the Earth Mother, the female powers of the universe and the elemental kingdoms. The stem represents the male powers of the universe and the plant kingdom. The stem is usually decorated with fur and feathers or leather representing the animal kingdom. When the bowl and the stem are joined together the pipe is sacred. The people use the pipe to make their prayers to the Creator. The smoke carries the prayers.

There are many different forms the pipe ceremony takes, depending upon how this sacred knowledge was given to the people of a particular area. However, no matter what form the ceremony takes, it is important that all participants are as centered and focused as possible, since everything you think and feel while the pipe is being smoked are a part of the prayers you are making.

The pipe is one of the most sacred and important medicine objects to my people. It should always be treated with great respect.

The Sweatlodge

The sweatlodge, also called the stone people's lodge, is a ceremony conducted to cleanse our bodies, minds, hearts, and spirits. By bringing together the four elements (earth, air, fire, and water) we create the breath of the grandfathers and grandmothers. Through sweating and praying we are able to clean our bodies of toxins, our minds of negativities, our hearts of hatred and all the feelings that come from hatred, and our spirits of doubt. This ceremony helps us come into a proper relationship with ourselves and everything around us.

The sweat is a powerful ceremony to keep us healthy, and for many native people it is the first line of defense in healing.

Sometimes, if we're working with a person for a specific illness, we might build a little sweatlodge just for that person. Depending on the illness a variety of herbs are burned on the sweat rocks. Sage and cedar are most frequently used but stinging nettle is specifically good for rheumatism or arthritis. It helps the inflammation go away.

The person who needs healing enters the sweatlodge and the water is poured on the rocks while serious prayers are made. Everyone in the sweat prays hard for the one needing the healing and, if possible that person prays hard for himself. This is called a healing sweat. It is the responsibility of the person being healed to pray to be healed, to ask that the healing energies come to him, and to ask spirit to let the medicine person heal him. Sweats are powerful for cleansing, focusing, healing yourself, healing your loved ones and your friends, and for healing the Earth Mother through prayer.

The Medicine Wheel

The Medicine Wheel is a sacred circle usually built from stones. The Medicine Wheel of my vision consists of thirty-six stones, each one representing a part of the universe. It is entered, with consciousness, for healing, giving thanks, praying, or meditating. There are circles similar to the Medicine Wheel built all over the world, creating healing for our Earth Mother and for ourselves. As more people learn about the old ways, new Medicine Wheels are being created and more of this type of healing is taking place.

The Medicine Wheel Ceremony is very ancient. I am always happy to build Medicine Wheels wherever I go as they improve the energy of the earth in whatever area they are constructed. At one time, there were some 20,000 Medicine Wheels in the United States and Canada alone. There were similar ceremonial circles in Mexico, India, all over Europe, and in many other locations. Stonehenge in England is a form of the Medicine Wheel. In Germany, after being brought to a sacred area, I was immediately able to identify not only a Medicine Wheel but also the ceremonies a shaman had performed there.

I was given my vision of the Medicine Wheel over a decade ago and have been teaching and sharing the ways of it ever since. More information on using the Medicine Wheel for healing can be found in my book, *The Medicine Wheel*. Here I want to share that the Medicine Wheel can be a powerful element in finding your path, your power, and guidance for your journey around the sacred circle that is your life. On one level, the Medicine Wheel teachings are part of a very old medicine. On another, they are the beginnings of the dance, and a connection to strong teachings on the earthly and physical levels. These teachings can help in healing you and in enhancing your perspective. They can also help you acknowledge your power and give you basic information and ideas for growth. The Earthstones are a further evolution of my original vision, as are Medicine Wheel Consultations which help people understand their own movement around the wheel. We give seminars to teach people how to do these. If you are interested, contact the Bear Tribe for times and requirements of the seminars.

The very advanced apprentices and those willing to come to certain levels of consciousness and power can experience a much deeper and stronger form of Medicine Wheel. These levels of consciousness embrace all of the circle of life and see everything in the circle as deeply connected. On this level, there are no barriers and all fears cease to exist. This form of medicine allows you to reach any level of consciousness. It is like a springboard for the medicine power path. At the point where everyone is doing the same dance of medicine, power, and union, experiences such as total mental telepathy and teleportation are possible. This is all that I can share in this book. If you are drawn toward this path then apprenticeship might be appropriate for you.

Vision Quest

One of the ways to find your medicine or your path of power is to go on a Vision Quest. You should be prepared for this by a medicine woman or medicine man, or a Vision Quest guide. Before you begin the actual quest, you or your guide will choose an area out in nature. The ceremony consists of fasting and praying for one to four days. It is also called "crying for a vision."

Your vision tells you who you are, what you are really supposed to do, what your highest good and goal should be, and gives you clarity about the meaning of life. There is a book we helped publish called *The Book of the Vision Quest*, by Steven Foster and Meredith Little, which tells about this sacred rite. We also set aside time for Vision Questing at the Bear Tribe in Spokane, Washington, and in other parts of the country. For the first couple of days you go through decontamination, which is getting free from energies that you have brought with you from the city and releasing the garbage you carry around. Next, there is a day for consulting with the guides about the Vision Quest and going out on the mountain to ready yourself further. The next day, you enter a sweatlodge doing prayer and ceremony. After that your earthly claim is considered released. From that point on you are considered of the spirit realm. You begin a period of silence. Then the guide brings you to your questing place.

During the quest you no longer exist in this world. Through ceremony, you are pushed to the spirit world and all the focus is on prayer and vision. After your Vision Quest, there may be another sweatlodge and the guide will help interpret your vision, if you want help.

The Vision Quest has always been a powerful ceremony for native people. It is becoming a very important ritual for many people of all backgrounds today. After you have found your true connection to the Earth Mother and all of life, you will be dancing your own dance. Once you have cried for your vision there is always something to carry you forward in life.

DREAMING

Dreaming is a very powerful way to learn what is good for you. Your dreams can give you important information. Before you go to sleep, balance yourself by focusing on what you want from your dreams. Take a moment to think about your day, clearing and releasing thoughts. Do you have questions about yourself, what's good for you, the future, or the past? Do you want to connect on deeper levels with your subconscious? Do you want to remember and understand your dreams better? Ask for what you need. Be clear.

Program a dream medicine object or a crystal to help you remember dreams. Hold it to your head, focus on it, then tell it your needs. Place your dream helper under your pillow or under your bed. Keep notes of your progress so you can see which dream recovery methods work best for you.

Your dream time is very important because it provides a way to reach the spirit world. It is a time when your busy little brain is taken out of its regular circuits, allowing you to explore other avenues of power. The Aborigines of Australia say they have 40,-000 years of dream history. They have a process of very strong healing they do in a dream state. They actually dream the healing.

When they reach a certain age in their youth, they go out on a special voyage called a Walkabout. It is done at a sacred area, such as the Ayers Rock, which used to be a favorite location. At this time, they live off the land completely in the old way. During the time of Walkabout, the focus is on dreaming and connecting with the spirit powers. Aborigines are very powerful in their knowledge of how to dream about something or someone and change the events or improve the health of the person they are dreaming about. They are known to dream their whole lives before they happen, and also to dream about the lives of their children. And this is how they travel from the past to the future. This is where much of their power lies.

I am a dreamer. Dreaming is one of my strong medicines, and much of my medicine comes to me through dreams. I delight in this, as I always feel good with the spirits. Sometimes my dreams come in sequences, each night another powerful continuation from the night before, teaching or giving me a long sequence of knowledge or information all on one subject. Other times I will have short, little dreams about many completely different things. With time, it becomes easier to determine what is a power dream and what are more subtle dreams. Before going to sleep at night, program yourself for what you want to work on, or for what guidance or direction you want from your spirit and dream guides.

There are special medicine objects that some native Americans use called dreamweavers or dreamnets. These catch the dream and hold it for you.

I always keep a notebook close to my bed so I can write down the good ideas that come to me from my dreams. You can do this too. When people ask me where I get some of my super ideas, I tell them very honestly, "I dreamed it up!"

Dream Travel

Traveling in a dream state can become a common occurrence. When I want to do this, I prepare myself by praying and focusing myself before I go to sleep. My two most frequent forms of dream travel are as an eagle or as a part of Brother Wind. The sky is the pathway for my journey. It's a very powerful experience to see all of the living Earth Mother below, or to feel and be a part of the wind.

Being the wind can be a wild and exciting feeling, like an unending flow of powerful emotion, or as gentle as a caress between loved ones. The wind has been my powerful ally in many situations. Because I travel with the wind in my dreams, a part of me is the wind and, at times, the wind will come when I call in a sacred way through prayer. This occurrence has been helpful for turning the heads of some participants at events who have been slow to grasp the power and reality of the medicine path. After a little wind storm they are usually convinced that other realities exist.

My greatest tool for my dreaming medicine is that I'm constantly in a state of preparation for it. I am always making a real effort in all my thoughts and actions to be prepared for dreams or visions that come, whether I'm asleep or awake. Some part of my focus is ready or preparing for this type of medicine at any given moment.

Sometimes, I go to people in their dreams if I need to communicate with them. One friend called me up and told me about her dream from the night before in which we met and spoke of important things having to do with her growth. When she was done I said, "I know this dream well, I was there, too." I do this by projecting myself out at the night. However, I do not encourage new dreamers to try this without help from a dream teacher or dream guide.

There was a friend who bought many of our magazines (now *Wildfire*, at that time called *Many Smokes*) for his booth at arts and crafts shows. He would never read them. He bought them and put them under the counter until he had about a two-year supply.

Eventually, he began having health problems and needed to get out of the city, away from the pollution and stress. But the idea of living in the country was foreign to him. He continued to take no action and his condition grew worse. Finally, I came to him in a dream. For four nights in a row I stood near the stack of magazines and just kept shaking my finger at him.

I didn't see him for a while. When I did run into him he said, "Sun Bear, Sun Bear, I've got to talk to you about what has happened to my life." He said his health had been bad and, though he knew leaving the city would help, he didn't know how. Then he had this dream four nights in a row. It shook him up so badly he sat down and read all the back issues of *Many Smokes*.

The magazines had so much good information about the Earth Mother and living outside the cities that they gave him the confidence he needed to move to the country. After his move, away from the pollution and stress, he regained his health. He also remained a faithful reader. So good things can come out of my dream travels.

Dreaming is a constant consciousness training that helps you to tune into all your senses and get in touch with your inner self and feelings. Dreaming can also help guide you, and even warn you, about some situations that could be dangerous. I'm alive today because of dreams that have warned me of life-threatening situations. One time, Wabun and I were getting ready to depart for a workshop in Hawaii. The night before we were to leave, I had a powerful dream that warned me not to go. I cancelled the trip. As it turned out there was a terrible hurricane where we would have been and the whole area was completely devastated. I still thank Great Spirit for that warning.

SPIRITUAL HEALING

There are many forms of spiritual healing, be it through prayer, psychic surgery, visualization, powerful sacred medicine, or other methods.

Some of the most well-known are those documented at Lourdes in France, a Catholic-based shrine where numerous healings have taken place. A row of crutches hangs from a wire stretched across a grotto. These are testimony to those no longer crippled and in need of their crutches. They have been healed by bathing in the water that flows from a spot where a vision took place many years ago. Thousands of people gather there daily and much healing takes place.

When I was in Frankfurt, Germany, a man came to me who had

been crippled for eleven years and had to use supports to walk. This man said, "Sun Bear, you are going to heal me." I replied, "Well, that's between you and Spirit if it is going to work." But I did a ceremony and prayed very hard over him. Afterward, he stood up and said, "I am well." His legs were completely healed. This was at a workshop with about seventy people. About ten of those people are now my apprentices, including some doctors and psychiatrists.

They saw something real happen. Some of them knew this man and his case history and knew that Spirit had responded, that these natural powers are real. Another time, outside San Francisco, a woman came to me with a big wide burn on her arm. She asked me to do a healing ceremony. Two M.D.'s who were working with me witnessed this healing ceremony. I started praying while focusing my attention on her arm, and the wound began to close up until it was about the width of my two fingers. At that moment, someone came into the room and called out my name. This broke my concentration and ended the healing. However, the burn was much smaller than it had been at the beginning of the ceremony.

These are powerful things and are not uncommon for medicine men and medicine women.

Medicine Men and Medicine Women

Medicine people are powerful men and woman who can heal in a sacred way on many levels. Some forms of healing they do are through ceremony and prayer. Other forms are through herbs, remedies, the Sacred Pipe Ceremony, Sweatlodge, sacred dances, Vision Quest, and more.

For thousands of years, the medicine people of native American tribes healed and guided their people in beautiful and powerful ways. They cared for the sick, healed the wounded warriors, birthed the babies, and spiritually guided the tribe as a whole.

Many medicine people are born with their power and then develop it through the years. Other medicine men and medicine women come into their power during their Vision Quest. They have powerful visions that tell them they are to be medicine people. Sometimes, it happens in one day. They are on their Vision Quest and the healing powers come to them, and they are able to heal.

Often, the elders shared their powerful range of healing information with a young person who seemed to have an interest or calling to heal. The young healer would apprentice to a specific medicine person, gaining practical knowledge about the use of herbs and remedies and learning the rituals and ceremonies that were given by the ancestors over many generations of knowledge. Much medicine is very practical. For instance, the Navaho people who become healers are also well-known for their ability to be able to find lost objects, a convenient power to have. There are some medicine people whose hands tremble when they heal. That is their particular gift, their medicine.

One thing I will caution you about. If you really want to walk the sacred path and you want to learn, always go with respect to any medicine man or medicine woman, or any teacher who works with these powers. Let me tell you a story that expresses what I want to share with you.

There was a Navaho medicine man who was blind. He was a strong healer and helped many people. One day, members of a family came for a healing. They brought him three sheep. When choosing the sheep they said, "Well, he is blind, let us choose our scrawniest, lowest grade sheep as he won't know the difference." When they arrived they said, "Please do this healing for us. We have brought you three sheep."

The medicine man did not inspect or handle the sheep in any way but proceeded directly with the healing. After he had finished the healing he said, "I have fulfilled my agreement with this healing. However, because you have knowingly brought me three sheep that were no good, for the next generations your family will die off very young and very rapidly." He said, "Eventually you will have no descendants." And what he said came true. I knew this family personally, and the last member of the family died five years ago, leaving no descendants.

One of the things about the power of this knowledge and this medicine is that the Spirit gives it to you. There are loving spirit helpers and protectors who are strong and powerful. This medicine is good and much good can come from it. However, it is important to realize there must be respect for this medicine and power or there can be repercussions.

Shamanism

The word *shaman* actually came from Siberia and means medicine man or medicine woman. The term medicine man or woman was given to us by the French because we healed people. To them, healers were people who practiced medicine. But many of us worked more with the spiritual/psychic/mental/emotional part of people or situations. Knowledge of this aspect can bring about much healing, so much so that I say, "Knowledge itself is healing."

I've done healing myself and I am a shaman. However, I don't claim to be a healer. I think of myself as a teacher. Teaching is my path and a fulfillment of my personal vision. Many of my apprentices are greater healers than I am. I don't believe you have to be everything. You are what you are capable of being. Many people automatically heal themselves as they learn to live with better feelings about themselves, with clearer feelings about the way the universe is, and with a stable balance in their lives. This creates the space for them to heal themselves.

There is a young man in this country named Brant Secunda. He has studied with a powerful healer and shaman down in Mexico named Don Jose. Don Jose is around 110 years old and still going strong, working along the path in a good way. His teachings are powerful, too. Brant is his student and from what he has learned he is capable of healing. One time, I went to Mexico and had been traveling and working very hard, creating an imbalance in my health. Brant did a strong healing on me, drawn from the knowledge Don Jose had taught him, and I bounced right back to my regular, powerful self.

Kahunas

A Kahuna is a person, usually of Hawaiian ancestry, who has grown into a level of spiritual consciousness that places him on the same level with many of the spirit powers and forces, so that he is able to communicate with them, and work with them on many levels, including healing. The Kahunas are very powerful healers. They are famous for healing severely injured people.

I know of a Kahuna who had a man bring his son to him. The child had been in an auto accident. He had broken ribs and his intestines were hanging out of his body. The Kahuna began praying and put his hands on him. The child's wounds closed, and, within four days, he was completely well.

Another friend of mine had a little dog that was run over by a car and was hurt so badly he barely had any of the life force left in him. She took the dog to a Kahuna. He prayed over the dog and restored his *mana* or life force energy. The dog regained perfect health. In chapter 5 I told you about some Kahuna brothers and sisters and their amazing powers. I told about working with the elements in Hawaii. It is common for the Kahunas to work with the elements. They have the power that works with the volcanoes, the winds and rains, and Grandfather Sun. The most beautiful, delicious fruits and foods grow in Hawaii. It is said that the islands are the Spiritkeepers' vacationlands, for it is so beautiful and the Spirit moves so freely there.

Psychic Surgeons

I know a healer from the Philippines who came to this country to do some specially requested healings. I watched him as he prepared himself that morning by going into a trance. He stayed in his trance all day long. I watched him as he prayed over the people who needed healing. I was with him and closely watched all that he did. He ran his hand down the back of one man who had had a serious chronic back problem for many years. I saw a growth imbedded in the flesh. The surgeon worked the growth loose and removed it with his fingers. Then he ran his hand over the area, closing the open wound, and the man was joyfully and gratefully healed.

Another man was brought in who appeared to be having a heart attack. He was ashen and slumped over, with beads of sweat on his brow. The psychic surgeon worked on him for about twenty minutes. The previously ill man came out and drove himself home. All through the day the surgeon performed many healings. This obviously was his calling and his special work for which he was here. At the end of the day, he told the people there "My powers are going away, I can't do any more healing now."

In many cases there are things you can't always explain but they do bring healing. Many of these healers work by praying for the spirits to bring the dis-ease together into one area where they can then draw it out of the physical body.

There is a man in Brazil called the "Little Beggar." He works only with people who have chronic and terminal illnesses. He will not take payment and consistently does complete healings on very sick people. Usually he only does them on Saturdays and Sundays because during the week he works as a barber. When he smells the odor of tobacco coming into the room while he's doing healing he knows he is done for the day. He says, "I have to stop now because the spirits won't let me do anymore today." This scent is the spirits' way of saying that his powers are going away until another day.

HEALING CENTERS

Alternative health comes in many forms. Fortunately, more and more types of alternative health care are available in this country. I am a very strong advocate of the concept of the healing center.

A healing center is a place where spiritual and ceremonial healings are combined with physical, mental, and emotional techniques. It is a place where a person will be treated with as much knowledge and compassion as my people used to be by their own medicine men and women.

In this new age of changes, the healing center is an option that is becoming somewhat more available as people desire to take responsibility for their own health and to participate in reaching their optimum well-being. The healing center gives people an opportunity to make and realize personal health and well-being goals.

The programs allow the participant to explore his dis-ease with the assistance of qualified practitioners and facilitators who have an abundance of healing abilities to draw from.

The programs at healing centers usually run from ten days to three months, with some having follow-up programs or refresher courses. Often patients will be given referrals to practitioners who are in their area and can continue to help them.

The basic programs usually include bodywork and other physical healing; specific food programs covering extensive nutritional counseling; emotionally therapeutic exercises for stress management and releasing energy blocks; and movement expression and exercise programs. The theory underlying healing centers is focusing your attention on your personal healing, while giving you a long-range maintenance program for living a full and balanced life.

Many of my apprentices are involved with the healing center

concept and with actual healing centers. See appendix A for more information.

Too often in our society people go to a doctor when they are already very sick or dying. It would be much more sensible for them to integrate a life long health plan into their lives that can keep them vibrant for years. People are not educated enough about the basic concept of good health. This education is a primary focus of healing centers, and of alternative healing.

10 | Other Natural Alternatives

One thing people have to be careful about is not becoming dogmatic. This applies even to New Age ideas of healing and lifestyle. People should be open to all ways of healing, including medical doctors. If it works, use it. If it will do the job and heal you, then you should be using it. If it solves the problem, if a person can get well from her illness, then it's good.

As I said before, I'm an advocate for healing centers. In a healing center a person is assessed from head to toe and then treatment is prescribed. In some cases fasting and cleansing is necessary, in others nutritional guidance or colonics, massage therapy, herbal remedies, acupuncture, homeopathy, sweatlodge ceremony, or stone therapy is needed. And there are times when there is no alternative but surgery or medically prescribed drugs. It is emotionally, physically, and financially challenging enough to be sick. You want to have as many options and tools as possible available to restore you to good health. I am not attached to the method; I am concerned with the results. The Creator put many different gifts upon the earth to learn from and use for healing. If you remain open to them, there is a much better chance of survival.

This chapter describes a variety of forms of healing on the physical, emotional, spiritual, and mental planes. This is not a comprehensive list. It is merely meant to give you some definitions of different healing methods that are available. Use it in conjunction with the resource guide in Appendix A to find the healing modalities that are right for you. To connect with additional methods of healing or facilitators and facilities that do these kinds of treatments in your area, look in your phone book, go to self-help, esoteric or New Age bookstores, or see if there is a local resource guide or newspaper with holistic and alternative health listings for your area. Look in the back of New Age and health magazines for organizations or clinics that advertise or are listed. Check with free clinics and colleges in your area. Sometimes women's self-help or health centers have listings. Alternative weekly newspapers have ads as do bulletin boards at places like health food stores, tai chi, dance, movement, or yoga centers. Ask friends and acquaintances. Word of mouth is an excellent way to find a good healer. Be a good detective and don't give up until you find the answers you are looking for.

Once you find some potential alternative health practitioners, your work is just beginning. You should then make a good effort to check these practitioners out. Just like psychic surgeons, some people in holistic health will be very good and some will be bad. I've met alternative healers of all types who are as dogmatic as many doctors. They think their method of healing—whether it is massage, colonics, psychology, or environmental allergy testing—is the only good method. I shy away from such people. I think most things will help someone at some time, but I haven't yet found one way of healing that works for everyone all the time. If I had, that's what I'd be doing.

When you first go to an alternative healer, ask her about her training, her course of therapy and her charges. Ask her for recommendations from people who have used her. Find out her philosophy of life and healing, and be sure that it is agreeable with yours. If you don't like someone, even if she is an excellent healer, she is unlikely to help you. If you really don't believe in a healer's philosophy and methods, go elsewhere. Doubts aid disease, not healing.

Some therapists and healers will give you a free or reduced rate introductory session or will make time to sit and talk with you. I always feel better about a healer who is willing to get to know me, and let me know something about her. Your health-care practitioners are your partners-in-health. It is important you feel good about each other.

HEALING MODALITIES
There are many different alternative modes of healing. Some deal with the physical body (e.g., nutrition, diet, vitamins, exercise, elimination, massage). Some deal with the mental body (e.g., posi-

tive thinking, affirmations, biofeedback). Others are concerned with the emotional being (e.g. gestalt, reevaluation counseling, orgonomy, bioenergetics, transpersonal psychology, humanistic psychology). Still others work with the spiritual aspect (e.g., schools and methodologies that work with one's relationship to the universe).

New methods of healing seem to be discovered, or rediscovered, with frequency today. Consequently, it is difficult to make a complete glossary of different forms of alternative healing. What follows is a listing of the holistic healing ways we know something about personally:

Aerobics. Aerobics is exercising to the point that heart and lungs are stimulated for a significant period of time, enabling the body to have a cathartic change in the cardiovascular system, in weight, in muscle tone, and in stamina. Contrary to popular belief, you do not have to have snazzy color-coordinated exercise clothes to do aerobic exercise. You can do aerobic exercise by dancing, swimming, bike riding, or running. Your clothing need only be comfortable, not designer quality.

Acupuncture. Acupuncture works to correct imbalances in the energy flow (also known as *chi*) so as to alleviate or prevent illness. The energy of the body circulates through what are called meridians. The body has hundreds of points that correspond with all organs and physical aspects. By stimulating the correct point with a very fine needle, energy balance can be restored. Diagnosis is done through a full examination of the patient, by taking the pulse and making an assessment of other factors such as emotions, the tastes a person is attracted to, tones of color coming from her face, what season it is, the skin temperature and texture, and other factors.

In China and Tibet, acupuncture has been used to cure almost every illness known to humanity. It is very popular of late for assisting in weight loss, quitting smoking, and alleviating pain such as migraines and backaches.

I have had good results with acupuncture and so has Crysalis. She had a large troublesome ovarian cyst removed surgically. About a year later, all the symptoms returned and another cyst demanded medical attention. Rather than opting for expensive and exhausting surgery, she used acupuncture. Within two weeks, all symptoms disappeared and there was no need for surgery.

Another friend of mine was extremely compulsive. After some encouragement, he went to see an acupuncturist to quit smoking. The results were so successful that he went back for weight-loss treatment. Since then he has lost significant weight and has not taken up cigarettes again.

Acupressure. Acupressure is similar to acupuncture, except it is a form of massage where points and nerves close to the surface of the body are stimulated through applied pressure instead of needles. This sends a message to the brain that can release painful elements, cure a variety of ailments and relieve tensions in the body. Acupressure can be good for relief from headaches, sports injuries, toothaches, menstrual cramps, arthritis, and other painful problems. This form of massage has been conducive to healing and curing a large variety of ailments, not just alleviating pain.

Affirmations. Affirmations are visualizations put into words. Affirmations are statements that are written or repeated at regular intervals to bring about desired changes in any aspects of a person's being.

Ayurvedic. Ayurveda, a sanskrit word which means "the science of life," has been practiced extensively in India for at least 5,000 years. It is one of the oldest recorded healing sciences in existence today, and encompasses the yogic philosophy and practice of healing and self-healing the body, mind, and spirit. Ayurveda regards the human being as a "living book." It is designed to correct organic imbalances in an effort to restore the innate harmony of the organism, and open it to the nourishing life source within and surrounding it. Close observation of this "book" in its physical, emotional, and spiritual aspects is considered carefully through analysis of the pulse, tongue, nails, eyes, and lips.

Bach Flower Remedies. Dr. Edward Bach stated that "disease should be cured not by attacking a specific illness or ailment but by restoring the natural harmonic balance of the patient, so that the body itself will reject disease." Drawn from the essence of wildflowers that come into bloom from the powers of the sun, the Bach Flower Remedies produce results which have astonished conventional M.D.'s. Through the administration of small doses of simply prepared tinctures of the flowers from trees and herbs, powerful healing has taken place for a vast variety of illnesses, from rheumatism, ulcers, and shock to depression and anxiety. Under Dr. Bach's system, the remedies can be used alone or in association with other forms of treatment, without interfering with them. Wabun has had many positive results with the Bach Flower Remedies, and with the floral essences produced by the Flower Essence Society in California.

Bioenergetics. Bioenergetics is a therapy that uses the language of the body to heal the problems of the mind. This body-mind approach to personality has a liberating and positive effect on emotional, physical, and psychic stress. Dr. Alexander Lowen, founder of this therapy, states that increased joy and pleasure are possible in everyday life through an understanding of how your body functions energetically; how it determines what you think, feel, and do. Physical ailments like headaches and lower back pain as well as emotional conflict can be relieved through bioenergetic exercises and therapy.

Biofeedback. Biofeedback is a method of making us aware of processes going on within our bodies and minds, through microelectronic equipment. It is used for teaching relaxation, and for controlling diseases largely caused by stress.

Chiropractic Care. Chiropractic care is the art of spinal manipulation. The goal is to relieve all pressure from the nerves that extend from the spine and connect to the various organs, thereby relieving stress, pain, and potential for disease. The nervous system is made up of the spinal cord, nerve branches, and the brain. So, through manipulation of the spine, proper and healing interaction can take place between the nervous system and the rest of the body. Frequently, chiropractors integrate other practices such as acupuncture, massage, physical therapy, diet, and nutrition.

Colonics. The colonic theory is that blockages and/or constipation of the colon can create serious toxicity, resulting in health problems such as headaches, colds, skin disorders, exhaustion, poor memory, nausea, and other various maladies. Some health-care practioners feel that the root of all disease stems from the colon.

Colonics, a high-tech form of enema, are the process of cleaning the large intestine with a special machine that regulates the flow and pressure of water entering through the rectum. Colonics should be done under the supervision of a doctor or qualified health practioner.

Color Therapy. Color therapy is the process of using specific color vibrations for balancing and healing the body. Color therapy stems from ancient practices. Certain colors are connected with healing certain illnesses. The colors predominately used are the colors of the rainbow, which correlate with each of the seven chakras. Each totem and spiritkeeper of the Medicine Wheel has a correlating color. These colors can be worked with to draw in the energies of the corresponding totem or spiritkeeper.

Crystal Healing. Crystal healing is any one of a large number of methods to bring about energy balance in the body. Most often clear quartz is used. Smoky quartz, amethyst, rutilated quartz, and rose quartz are also frequently used.

Dowsing. Dowsing is a method of finding water, or almost anything else, through the movement of a pendulum or of dowsing rods. This time honored method of finding water is also used today to find power places, energy lines, and movement of energy in the human body.

Earthstones. Earthstones are a method of self-understanding and finding one's path of power through using stones based upon my vision of the Medicine Wheel.

Fasting. Fasting is the process of abstaining from food. This process can be conducive to eliminating toxins or poisons from the body and as a spiritual catalyst in journeys such as the Vision Quest. It can be potentially dangerous if not supervised by a health-care practioner or spiritual guide.

Feldenkrais Method. By practicing the Feldenkrais Method, which teaches awareness through movement or functional integration, harmony of action can flow with ease and efficiency. After integrating this method, people who have had problems touching their toes can sometimes touch their foot to their forehead. The method was developed by Moshe Feldenkrais, an Israeli engineer and physicist whose own knee injury started him on a quest to understand human movement and body consciousness.

Gestalt Therapy. This is a psychology that tries to help individuals discover their own inner teacher through their life patterns, behaviors, dreams, and relationships. The therapy was developed by Fritz Perls, one of the founders of the humanistic psychology movement. Gestalt attempts to teach people to live in the present moment.

Herbalogy. Herbalogy is the study and use of herbs. Since early in human history, herbs have been used to eat, to spice, and to heal. The use of herbs for healing continues today in most parts of the world. In the United States, however, the Food and Drug Administration attempts to limit the use of herbs that make any claims to medicinal properties. Herbalogy is discussed in more detail in chapter 9.

Homeopathy. Homeopathy is a system of medical practice that treats disease with minute doses of a remedy that would, in healthy persons, produce symptoms of the disease treated. The basic theory is, *similia similibus curentur*—"like cures like." Samuel Hahnemann is the founder of modern homeopathy. While frowned upon by many contemporary American doctors, they utilize a homeopathic principle when they inoculate people against smallpox, polio, and a variety of other diseases.

Hypnosis. Hypnosis is an induced state that resembles sleep. In it, the subject is particularly responsive to suggestions. This process has proven to be helpful in losing weight, stopping smoking, and in a variety of other situations.

Iridology. This is the science of diagnosis of the eyes. Every organ and part of your body is represented in your iris. The practitioner's procedure upon examination is to note unusual lines or changes of hue in the iris. This reveals the location of illness or dysfunction within the body. By studying and evaluating the eyes, illnesses can be diagnosed and therefore treated.

Macrobiotics. The macrobiotic diet is low-fat, low-protein, complex-carbohydrate, and high fiber. It consist of 50 percent to 60 percent grains, 25 percent vegetables, 10 percent sea vegetables and beans, 5 percent soup and occasional fish. Its purpose is to bring the body into balance by eating whole foods, grown locally and in season. The macrobiotic diet is not static; it is tailored to each individual's present conditions and needs. Macrobiotics helps in understanding the energy of the universe, from foods to cosmological influences.

Massage. Massage is the art of manipulating the body through pressure and motion to create harmony, health, and relaxation. Swedish massage, rolfing, reflexology, shiatsu, acupressure, Alexander Technique, esalen, polarity therapy, orthobionomy, Feldenkrais, trager, and postural integration are all contemporary message methods.

Naturopathy. Doctors who practice naturopathy allow the patient's body to heal itself with a minimum amount of unnatural intervention, especially pharmaceutical drugs. Instead, they utilize such techniques as massage, herbs, hydrotherapy, mineral baths, exercise, spiritual manipulation, nutrition, fasting, homeopathy, and other natural alternatives.

Orgonomy. Orgonomy is the science developed by Wilhelm Reich, a physician, psychoanalyst, and scientist. Physical orgone therapy is the use of various orgone energy devices, particularly the orgone accumulator, to treat physical illnesses. It is strictly experimental and, since shortly before Reich's death, hasn't been used in an organized way by the medical profession to treat illness. Experimentation on animals using these devices is continuing through the American College of Orgonomy. The results of these studies are published in the *Journal of Orgonomy*.

Psychiatric orgone therapy is a method for the treatment of emotional disorders developed by Wilhelm Reich which includes attention to states of chronic muscular tension (armoring) in the body, and the analysis of character, as well as the usual approaches of psychotherapy.

Orthobionomy. This is a method of dealing with acute and chronic pain, emotional release, and structural alignment, without the use of force or manipulation. Homeopathic in application, it integrates the body, mind, and spirit. Through gentle, relaxing movements and comfortable postures, the body is eased into positions that unblock tensions and release stressful muscular patterns.

Osteopathy. Osteopathic medicine is a system of health care founded by Andrew Taylor Still (1828–1917) and based on the theory that the body is capable of making its own remedies against disease and other toxic conditions when it is in normal structural relationship and has favorable environmental conditions and adequate nutrition. It utilizes generally accepted physical, pharmacological, and surgical methods of diagnosis and therapy, while placing strong emphasis on the importance of body mechanics and manipulative methods to detect and correct faulty structure and function.

Past Life Reading. This is a process of exploring oneself by retrieving information from past lives. This should be done with a therapist, who serves as a guide and helper in channeling and integrating the information received from previous incarnations. Frequently, this process is helpful in solving current problems and conflicts resulting from unresolved past life experiences.

Polarity Therapy. Dr. Randolph Stone, the founder of polarity therapy, described the therapy as follows: "This life energy flows around the body and through every cell in a predictable pattern, creating a 'wireless anatomy,' which can be stimulated when the energy flow becomes blocked. Polarity therapy does not treat disease or even specific organs; it is designed to re-establish the body's natural energy flow which allows the body then to heal itself. It accomplishes this through gentle manipulative techniques, combined with improvements in diet and nutrition, polarity, yoga exercises, and a more positive and loving attitude toward oneself and life."

Rebirthing. Rebirthing has been said to accomplish major emotional breakthroughs and releases. Through the assistance of a facilitator, relaxation, and breathing exercises, sometimes utilizing warm water flotation tanks, a rebirthing can take place. The breakthroughs and releases of rebirthing frequently have to do with experiences from one's birth or earliest childhood, or from past lives. These memories are brought to the surface through the exercises.

ReEvaluation Counseling. Reevaluation counseling is the process of releasing oneself from chronic patterns. It also helps confront the challenge of oppressive patterns from society and the universal distress of "powerlessness." A short and very inexpensive initial class gives you the skills and basics on how to counsel and allow yourself to be counseled. There are numerous people who have made these preparations and are available to share these skills. You can counsel for five minutes, an hour, or however long you wish, the crucial point being that each person takes an identical amount of time. All participants know the ground rules, thereby allowing a fair, loving, and supportive system of reciprocal growth and counseling to occur. This type of processing is being used not only by white middle-class intellectuals, but also by working-class communities, Blacks, Asians, young people, old people, Latinos, and women's groups.

Reflexology. Reflexology is an ancient method of healing through applying pressure to key areas of the body, especially reflex points on the hands and feet. The theory of reflexology is that each part of the body relates to a point on the foot or hand. Massaging these pressure points is beneficial for relaxation and cleansing. This method is excellent for stopping pain and helping the body heal itself.

Reiki. Reiki is an ancient healing art that traces its origin back at least 5000 years. It allows you to tap, at will, the higher frequency of natural cosmic energy and direct it to promote healing; reduce stress; build concentration; increase energy or relaxation; balance the mental, physical, emotional, and spiritual bodies; and remove deep seated causes that block higher potential, promoting peace, serenity, compassion, love, and wholeness.

Rolfing. Rolfing is a very deep massage that can break up physical and energy blockages and help to realign the body. Developed by Ida Rolf, a biochemist, rolfing helps to soften the connective tissues that have become tense in an effort to hold the body in a poor postural position. During Rolfing sessions, people may become aware of the original tensions or situations which caused their physical misalignments.

Sufism. Sufism is the mystical side of the Islamic religion. Parts of it have been brought to the contemporary Western world largely through the teaching of G. I. Gurdjieff, Pir Vilayat Inayat-Khan, and Reshad Feild. Sufism is a way to higher consciousness, rather than a set of religious principles. It can include techniques that range from quiet contemplation to the ecstatic dancing of the dervishes.

Tai Chi Chuan. Tai Chi Chuan is an ancient oriental art and moving meditation used for self-defense, agility, well-being, centering, relaxation, health, and harmony. It is dance-like in its flowing series of movement, and can be gently exhilarating. Tai Chi Chuan can be a catalyst to balance, coordination, and a healthy physique and spirit.

Therapeutic Touch. This is a healing art that you can learn to use simply by reading the book *The Therapeutic Touch: How to Use Your Hands to Help or Heal* by Dolores Krieger, Ph. D., R.N. It can be used to relieve everything from abdominal cramps, headaches, or muscle spasms, to soothing a crying baby. With this process, it is possible to detect when a person is sick, pinpoint where the pain is, and stimulate the recuperative powers of the sick person. Therapeutic Touch recaptures a simple, ancient mode of healing.

Touch for Health. Touch for Health is a variety of safe, simple, easy-to-use techniques which stem from chiropractic and from the modern practice of ancient oriental techniques. They are also called Applied Kinesiology. Balancing the structural, chemical, and spiritual and psychological aspects of a person is encouraged through methods such as muscle testing, structural awareness, meridians, oriental philosophy, muscle balancing, theory of the five elements, nutrition, allergy testing, acupressure, and massage. These methods are good for such problems as arthritis, bursitis, disc problems, menstrual problems, headaches, digestive disorders, and other acute as well as chronic health issues.

Traeger. Traeger is a form of deep tissue massage in which the body is realigned through a gentle rocking movement.

Transpersonal Psychology. Transpersonal psychology is concerned with the relationship between the individual and the cosmos, with conscious and unconscious mental levels, and with the collective unconscious. This therapy is also concerned with the shadow side of being of both people and the society. Any therapy which goes beyond the problems of the person to the person's link with the collective consciousness could be considered transpersonal.

Visualizations. Visualizations are a method of connecting the various aspects of being. Through holding a picture of positive change in their minds, some people are able to bring about healing, changes in thought or emotional patterns, or changes in the autonomic functions of the body. The Simonton method of cancer care utilizes visualizations and relaxation along with conventional remedies, as do other contemporary methods of healing.

Yoga. Yoga means to "join together" or "union" which is what it is about. Yoga joins the mental, physical, and spiritual through a variety of disciplines ranging from yoga asanas, which are a variety of physical postures, to breathing techniques. Yoga can also include diet, meditation, and philosophy. This is a multidimensional discipline that generates agility, good health, spiritual harmony, and strong physical well-being.

11 | What If You Get Sick?

I thank the Creator every day for keeping me as healthy as I am. Sure, being around my sixth decade of life, I've had various aches and pains, and a couple of bouts with illness, but, for the most part, I've been very fortunate. Having a good connection with Spirit, and knowing the amount and variety of healers I do, I've been able to use preventive or alternative health care most of the time. However, I go to allopathic health-care people when I want to check something out, as they are good with diagnosis, and with a variety of other problems. My disagreement with medical doctors is that many of them think their way is the only way. It's not. Often medicine people become the court of last resort for people who are ill. I've seen a number of "unexplainable" cures on people whom the docs had doomed to death. I always tell people never to accept the death verdict.

As Crysalis says, "While there's breath, there's hope." She knows that from the experience of having been seriously ill on a number of occasions. So do Wabun and Sentinel Bear, who also have had a couple of bouts with doctors and hospitals. I am relying on their experience and advice for much of this chapter. They tell me serious illness can be painful, frightening, inconvenient, expensive, frustrating, and lonely.

It is a very private place that is difficult for outsiders to comprehend. Understanding the foe is half the battle. All the pressures and agonies you might feel are circumstantial. They are symptomatic of the event of illness. If the symptoms are bad, you may feel terrible. It is important to remember you are not terrible. Your health challenges cannot alter the truth that you are inherently good. No matter how rotten you feel, you are still wonderful, human, sacred, and worthy. Too often, the dregs of being ill alter our self-esteem and sense of worth. This often causes us to feel guilty and blame ourselves for our health issues. There is a difference between taking responsibility for yourself and beating yourself up emotionally with guilt and blame. Guilt and blame resolve nothing. As I often say, guilt is the most useless emotion. Being responsible and focused evokes solutions and emotional stability in the midst of stress and upheaval.

Depending on your background and beliefs, if you become sick you go to a doctor or to some other kind of healer. No matter whom you approach, they all do two things that are the same. First, they name the problem. This is a critical step in healing. It gives you something to fight. It makes the unnamed thing knowable. What name the healer gives the problem depends upon their training and philosophy. A doctor will name an infectious agent (bacteria, viruses, etc.), immunological disease process, or structural abnormality. A shaman might find a substance placed in you by a person or force with whom you're having problems. I might tell you that you really are letting your ex-husband or wife make you sick. A spiritual healer might find a hole in your aura.

What is important in this naming is that you really believe in the same philosophy as your healer. If you have grown up thinking only doctors cure illness, it's going to be hard for you to get well by having a substance removed by a shaman or an aura hole fixed by a healer. Conversely, if you've grown up believing in spiritual healing, it is unlikely that allopathic medicine will make you well. You must believe in the method of healing you use.

Sure, you can change your belief system as you learn to do your own dance, but you are under enough strain being sick. Work on changing your beliefs when you are feeling better. Quite a few years back, an herbal healer was living with the Bear Tribe. This woman believed that everything was a cleansing crisis, and that you should go through it, assisted by herbs and enemas.

Also living at the Tribe was a woman who had been a doctor's wife. She got a real bad sore throat. The herbal healer insisted it was a cleansing crisis, and treated her accordingly. The other woman got worse to the point where she could hardly swallow. Finally I took her to the emergency room of the local hospital, where they said she was getting diptheria and gave her some powerful antibiotics which cured her. If I hadn't butted in, she could have been cleansed to death. Now it's possible that, with the exact same illness, the other woman would have been cured with herbs and enemas. She believed it was possible and that belief, along with the curing powers of the herbs, may well have done the trick.

CLARIFY CONFUSION

The second thing all healers do is give you a repetitious series of sounds or words you must repeat to yourself. This can be anything from a chant to instructions such as "Take one tablet an hour before meals. Do not use dairy products while taking this medication." This mantra helps the healing work by reminding you that you are taking steps to fight the enemy illness.

Confusion is one of the biggest problems people face when they are ill. Even if they believe only in allopathic medicine, there are still a number of different options to consider in the case of most treatments. It is really important that you ask to have all options fully explained to you. It is your body, and your life. You have a right to know all the choices available, and their probable consequences.

For example, a friend of ours went to the doctor because of excessive menstrual bleeding, a fairly common problem. She tried several medications, but they didn't help. Reluctantly, she agreed to a sonnagram. It showed a large mass on one ovary. Because she was over thirty-five, the doctor recommended a hysterectomy regardless of whether or not the mass was cancerous. She felt he was being knife happy, and agreed to have the mass removed, but not to have the hysterectomy unless the mass was malignant. It wasn't.

However, after the surgery the excessive bleeding continued. In fact, it became worse. Eventually, after a year of bleeding that reduced the blood in her body to half of what it should be, she was diagnosed as having endometriosis of the uterus and ended up having a hysterectomy.

My friend says that had she been told that the bleeding might have been coming from a uterine problem and not just the cyst, she would have been more open to considering a hysterectomy to begin with. But the doctors told her that they only think about the most serious condition first; they remove that, and hope it cures the problem.

In the course of the year between operations my friend did a lot of research about excessive bleeding. She probably had more up-to-date information than many gynecologists. She found that some doctors got angry at her because she had studied her own condition and wanted to have as much understanding as possible about what was happening with her body.

When she finally found a doctor who tried the least radical method first, and seemed like a gentle, decent person, she continued to see that doctor. When she had to have him perform the second surgery, she found that she healed much faster than she had from the first. Besides being willing to discuss options with her, this doctor also respected her desires about treatment and medication directly after surgery. She had read that being given sufficient pain medication right after an operation—enough that the body doesn't get in the habit of being in pain—often means taking pain medication for a much shorter period of time. It worked so well for her that she was out of the hospital three days after the operation, when she usually would have been hospitalized two or three days beyond that.

This woman's experience points out some of the problems in dealing with regular medical people. Often, doctors, being more knowledgable about medicine than patients, feel they shouldn't have to bother explaining their actions to their clients. True, a medical education is a long and expensive process. But so is apprenticing to a medicine person. Both make you knowledgable in certain areas. Neither makes you superhuman, or provides an excuse for arrogant or rude behavior. Don't buy into the medical mystique. It is true that doctors and nurses do important, life changing work, but so do teachers, farmers, and garbagemen.

It is critical that you have a doctor you feel good about, whether you are following a largely allopathic or holistic medical approach. If you have an accident or crisis, the only person most hospitals will recognize is a medical doctor or doctor of osteopathy. If you haven't found one you like, you're going to be stuck with whomever they give you. This could prove to be a very serious problem. There are good physicians out there, but you have to find them yourself. This is easier to do when you are well. Here are some suggestions to find a doctor who suits you.

Tips for Finding a Doctor

1. Be clear on what you are looking for. Do you want a doctor that reminds you of Marcus Welby, M.D., and a demigod? Be honest. Some people prefer a doctor who tells them what to do and how to do it. Or would you prefer more responsibility for your own medical care? Do you want a traditional doctor, or one with a holistic approach?
2. Take your time in choosing a physician.
3. Ask friends for recommendations.
4. Check the doctor's credentials with the local medical association, a hospital, or a physician's referral service. Nurses are also a wonderful source of information about doctors. They have both seen and heard how they practice medicine. Most attorneys who practice malpractice law also have computer lists of any suits brought against a doctor. A national list of such suits is available in some areas.
5. Talk to the potential physician. See if she treats you in the way you want to be treated. Do you feel respected as a human being? Will she answer your questions? Will she take time to listen? Does she explain herself well? Does she seem to be up-to-date on current medical knowledge? Most important, do you have a feeling of trust for this person?

You will stay healthier and heal faster if you are working with someone you like and trust. Remember, this person could literally hold your life in her hands at some point.

If it ever looks like you might be hospitalized, modify the above hints to help you choose a hospital. There are large differences in hospitals. When looking at one, be sure to check the nurse-to-patient ratio. You'll be seeing more nurses than doctors. If they are overworked, your care will suffer.

Become knowledgable about any medical problems you encounter. Doctors simply don't have the time to read everything. You might find something that could change the course of your own medical treatment.

If you need surgery, be particularly knowledgable. If at all possible, plan ahead so you have time to make peace with the operation, and to say a goodbye to whatever part of your body you are losing.

Things will go much smoother if you build yourself up ahead of time with good diet, rest, exercise, vitamins, and thoughts.

Plan to have a relative or friend act as your personal patient advocate if you are hospitalized. When you are sick or heavily medicated, it is good to have someone watching that things are done right. They make mistakes in hospitals. Ask any honest doctor or nurse. Some mistakes are silly. Others are deadly. Be sure your advocate knows what you want in as many situations as possible. If your condition is likely to become critical, be sure your advocate and your physician both know just what you want in heroic measures, and be as honest as possible. Don't tell someone you just want them to pull the plug unless you really mean it. Don't let illness or depression do your talking for you.

Pick an aggressive person as your advocate. He'll be coming up against medical egos. Be sure he has a healthy ego himself.

Following is a checklist of healing tips, taken from the experience of my coauthors and other friends, to help you through your illness.

Healing Hints

1. Find a support group, or a group of really supportive friends.
2. Talk about your illness whenever possible. This means whenever you feel you are in a safe, supportive environment. If you keep your worries inside, they create more mind creatures that can help keep you sick.
3. Doctors frequently are not emotionally supportive. If you have one that is, hang on to her. She is a rare gem. In recent times this has begun to change as people have demanded a more emotionally supportive medical system, and no longer take their doctor's word as that of an all-powerful diety force. However, science whiz kids are mainly the ones who get into medical school. Once there, they get pitifully little education about human nature—their own or other people's.
4. It is always appropriate and wise to get a second opinion. Many insurance companies now pay for this.
5. Although some physicians will not encourage implementing or opting for natural alternatives, it is your final decision, not theirs. They have a responsibility to give you your options to

the best of their medical ability. But it's always your choice as to what advice to follow, and what other avenues to pursue for your own healing. Don't be intimidated by your doctor. If you are, change doctors.

6. Many people have also followed the pendulum swing too far in the other direction and are reluctant to follow the advice of health care people who are not holistic. In some cases, there can be no other available alternative than surgery or medications. There is no glory in dying inopportunely, or in losing strategic bodily functions because of a prejudice against the A.M.A. Do what you have to do and don't wait too long to do it. Remember, the idea is to get well, not to make a dogmatic religion out of your beliefs in who should heal you or how you should be healed.

7. Research your health problem so you have information on what your options are. Read whatever you can find (go to libraries, bookstores, medical centers, etc.) so that you know your choices and options.

8. Keep in mind that most people will not know how to respond to your illness in a way that feels sympathetic to your needs. Many people will be in denial or feeling helpless, or will be so afraid for you that they will try to explain away your problem in order to make themselves more comfortable. Comments such as, "Oh, you'll be okay. It could be worse. I'm sure you'll be just fine. Don't worry. Don't think about it, etc." sometimes will make you feel worse. Be patient, if possible, and explain to the person that what would make you feel far better (if this is the case) is to express the fears and discomfort. Tell him you'd like to talk if he can handle it. Tell him you don't want to pretend everything is just peachy or will be just fine.

   The truth is that illness is usually uncomfortable, scary, expensive, inconvenient, and stressful. If someone is feeling really lousy and you're up to it, let them release their feelings and don't be so quick to "cheerful" it away. It can feel very invalidating to the ill person. I am not suggesting that you worship your pain or dis-ease. However, you do have a right to acknowledgment and support during a health crisis.

9. If someone repeatedly brings you an energy negative to your healing process, do not allow them access to you again until

you are well. Perhaps you should even consider why you'd allow them access then.

10. Decide on the best course of action for your healing process and stick to it. Be willing to change course, however, if the situation changes.
11. Watch your diet, the amount of sleep you get, your fluid intake, and your stress level.
12. Evaluate your exercise program for what is appropriate for your health problem. Sometimes less is wise. In other cases exercise will help.
13. Being ill can be traumatizing. Be respectful of what this means to you or to an ill friend or relative.
14. Don't overdo or rush to take on too much.
15. Returning to regular activity too soon is the overachiever's way to win a seat back in the doctor's office.

Before ending this chapter, I'd like you to think about what illness means to some people in this society. Health problems mean physical discomfort, challenge, and emotional stress for everyone. But for some people illness also means large debt. Dealing with the upheaval and inconvenience that can come with illness are difficult experiences in any case. Financial problems make it even worse.

Frequently it is impossible to work for undetermined lengths of time. Even with health insurance, many people cannot afford to cover overhead and bills while they are going through a health crisis.

The health care crisis in society is very complex. It involves millions of Americans and is most traumatic for the poor, the old, and the uninsured. These are the people who have the least options.

Good preventive medical care is still the privilege of people with money. Prevention is the key factor in avoiding illness and the financial burden associated with it. Unfortunately, it is the poor and many people in the middleclass who cannot afford or don't realize they should have checkups, medical tests, blood panels for cholesterol and triglyceride readings, blood pressure monitoring, high quality foods, medications, vaccinations for their children, or good prenatal care. Being concerned with these aspects of health care, and doing what you can to help, is another way of taking power over your life and of helping to heal the circle of life.

12 | Healing the Earth, Healing Ourselves

Humanity could become a short-term investment; the earth is long-term.

The treatment and condition of the earth today is something that my native people don't accept or fully understand. It goes against the code of life and is suicidal by its very nature. None of us can become fully healthy unless we do our part to help heal the planet.

Native people learned long ago that it is best to listen to nature and Spirit and respect the messages given us. In the Southwest, there were great cities at one time. In Chaco Canyon you can see the remains of a city with a population of more than 25,000 people. These people were told to move by Spirit. They listened and saw the signs that nature and Spirit gave them, and they moved. They knew that Spirit and nature gave them this warning because they knew how to look at nature and respect the earth.

The Earth Mother now has been giving mankind many signs about the earth changes. Even the World Almanac and the U.S. Department of Weather statistics show an increase in weather changes in recent years, such as hurricanes, typhoons, blizzards, serious storms, floods, and tidal waves.

I mourn when I see the stupidity of humanity regarding the earth. At one time in the Northwest, up in Oregon and other areas, they had great forests. The early settlers wanted these areas for farming, so they set fire to thousands of acres of magnificent pine and fir trees, destroying these monuments of life that took years to grow to their beauty.

They torched thousands of acres of trees to clear the land for farming. Because of their ignorance of the balance of nature, they would then wear out the farm land. In a short period of time, the once fertile land lay barren because of improper usage and no effort to refurbish the soil properly.

In all of life, if you take, you must give back. Some early settlers wore out the land by not giving back. These settlers would use up one farm and then move westward because of the destruction they created and would leave behind.

Not much has changed since those days, except there is no longer any place new to move on our planet. Sadly, little has been learned from past mistakes, at least by those in power.

In a similar fashion, but on a much larger scale, the rain forests are now being destroyed at over fifty acres per minute. These forests produce the plants for many lifesaving drugs, and provide shelter for a large number of the world's species of wildlife.

According to the *Gaia Peace Atlas*, edited by Dr. Frank Barnaby, there used to be about 1,500 million hectares of standing rain forest. Only 900 million remain today, and they are being destroyed at the rate of 11 million hectares each year. It is estimated that a species of wildlife goes extinct in the rain forests between every sixty seconds and every hour. These forests have generated about 50 percent of the world's rainfall by returning moisture to the air. As they are cut down, the planet dries up.

According to many experts now widely quoted in the media, the rain forest destruction plus other pollutants and emissions help to create acid rain and contribute to the Greenhouse Effect.

In the Antarctic a 100-mile-long and 60-mile-wide piece of ice has broken free in a melting process that is causing drastic changes. In 1988, the hole in the ozone layer was at least 15 percent bigger than in any earlier year. The ozone is in dire need of protection. To accomplish this, the manufacture of chlorofluorocarbon products (mainly found in styrofoam and aerosols) must stop. The laws are changing, but too slowly. Styrofoam cartons are what much fast food is packaged in. The cattle which produce the beef for the fast food companies is what the majority of the rain forests are being cut to accommodate. By writing to or boycotting fast-food companies that use Styrofoam containers or beef from the rain forests, you might help heal the ozone layer.

We've dumped our pollutants and garbage into the oceans. Now it is coming up on our shores. There are many places where the water table is completely contaminated. In another few years, without some drastic changes, water is not going to be fit for anyone to drink. You can't eat a fish over five pounds from certain rivers in Canada because they have too much pollution in them from the rivers.

RESIST THE DESTRUCTION
Each of us makes a choice either to assist or to resist in destroying the delicate balance of nature that makes life on our planet possible.

As we destroy the earth and our atmosphere, we destroy ourselves. Yet most people don't see this. I think it is largely because it is difficult to see how we each play a significant role in the whole of things as we lead our daily lives.

We have polluted our planet, and now we are looking to outer space for new frontiers so we don't have to reap what we've sown. Well, this is not a disposable planet. The Earth Mother is all we have, and the sooner we realize this, the better chance there will be for our survival.

Perhaps, because we've lived with all this for so long, many people don't seem to take seriously these and other problems, such as chemical and air pollution. According to the Environmental Humanity Documentary Slide Show, prepared by the Nurture Nature Program in Los Angeles, California, in 1987, 90 percent of all air pollution is invisible. Only 10 percent of all pollution is visible to the human eye no matter how gray the sky may appear. Smog causes damages costing at least twenty-five billion dollars a year. Yet, it has been estimated it would cost only nineteen billion dollars to clean most of it up.

Nuclear and hazardous wastes are another area that should be of tremendous concern to us all. Poisonous, destructive wastes have been dumped in landfills, sewers, lagoons, ponds, roads, ordinary incinerators, and the ocean. Hazardous wastes do not stay put when disposed of unsafely. They insidiously seep out into our environment. There is some form of toxic, hazardous, chemical, or nuclear waste inefficiently stored within fifty miles of every populated area in America and in most other cities of the world. More waste is in the "unpopulated" areas.

A partial list of the deadly effects of hazardous and nuclear wastes and chemical pollution are cancer, birth defects, radiation sickness, bone marrow destruction, blood disorders, immunologic disorders, hair loss, vomiting, nausea, diarrhea, and kidney and respiratory malfunction.

The statistics show that the number of toxic accidents are becoming increasingly rampant. Pesticides were found in the drinking water in Tennessee. Toxic fumes were sent into the air of New Jersey when abandoned chemical storage drums exploded. The James River in Virginia was contaminated with highly carcinogenic chemicals. Two hundred forty homes were evacuated in Niagara Falls due to toxic wastes. And of course, major "newsworthy" incidents such as Three Mile Island, Chernobyl, and the thousands dead in India from the Bhopal chemical disaster occasionally continue to bring the problems into public view.

Four of the biggest weapons plants in America are the Hanford facility in Washington; the Savannah River plant in Aiken, South Carolina; the plutonium processing plant near Boulder, Colorado; and the craftily named Feed Materials Production Center in Fernald, Ohio, which actually went so far as to paint checkerboard squares on one of the buildings so local residents would think it was a grain company. In common to all four places is the ill-health and loss of life brought to citizens in the surrounding areas because of the pollutants.

While the government might eventually close these facilities, it seems unwilling to take responsibility for the horrible suffering they've caused. People who've lost limbs to cancer, and have long winding scars on necks from thyroid operations are commonplace in these areas. The Hanford plant, alone, has created enough low-level waste to cover Manhattan. Most of the waste has been spilled into ponds, lakes, pits, and basins in the area.

Most frightening of all, is that there is, as yet, no proven safe means of storage or disposal of these nuclear wastes. But that has not stopped our government from producing them.

A GHOSTLY TRIBUTE
Not all of the poisonous chemicals on the earth have been directly put there by governments. Industry has done its fair share. So has farming.

Then there are true accidents. For instance, the innocent downfall of Times Beach, a town in the Midwest, was naively orchestrated by a man who thought he was doing a public service by spraying the streets with pesticide to keep the mosquitos down.

The whole town is closed down permanently, or for 25,000 years, whichever comes first, due to dioxin poisoning from this spray. Because a citizen could buy and use this chemical, which was not properly regulated by our government, the mosquitos are now the inheritors of this town. Rows of homes and buildings sit empty as a ghostly tribute to this serious blunder. Still, many people can't face the truth of it.

Many St. Louisians, who border the town of Times Beach, are oblivious to the serious nature of the disaster that has occurred. The government does not readily make available detailed, long-range statistics on the implications of a disaster of this kind. They seemingly discourage press coverage. Officials refrained from giving facts and future risk factors involved. Later, they denied many connections between Times Beach and the high incidence of cancer and other debilitating illnesses in the area. Frequently, the general rule of thumb for the government officials involved in these types of crisis situations, is to downplay it and hush it up as soon as possible.

Crysalis, who was born and raised in St. Louis, has many stories to tell of friends and relatives who are not being told by local physicians about the possible common origin of their emerging health problems from this, and from other environmental factors. The members of one family, who are friends of Crysalis, and live across the river from Times Beach, have developed strange lumps and tumors. Their doctors are only willing to say that the growths are highly toxic and shouldn't be altered in any way through surgery or injury as the contents are extremely poisonous.

Crysalis's prior family history has little sign of any cancer. However, at this time at least four members of her clan have had some form of this disease.

Unfortunately, only time, future deadly statistics and more heartbreaking catastrophies may help publicize the truth about this town, as well as other similar situations across the country.

Only education and publicity may make the facts believable to those individuals who still think today's current state of hazardous chemical exposure does not effect them, and is not an issue every-one should address. This continual denial of all these types of tragedies will escalate the actuality of the earth changes. The more people communicate to the governments of the world their feelings about these problems, the sooner regulations will go into effect that will protect the earth and us all.

PREPARING FOR CHANGE

I'm told by Spirit that the more people who change, the less severe some of the earth changes will be, but they will still come. Know-ing this, on a personal level, I like to be prepared for anything. This is what I do to maintain myself: Wherever I am, I have a basic amount of survival tools available. Because I travel so much this is limited, but I'm usually travelling to or from being with people of my beliefs who are well equipped with survival tools and rations. Still, I always have the necessities with me such as my can opener, a knife, a flashlight, and a can of sardines. These are my very basic survival tools.

Most people, however, should project out and have tools that will really help them survive over time. I suggest people always have at least five days worth of food and water in plastic containers. Always keep a full tank of gas, and a sleeping bag, flashlight, batteries, can opener, and some provisions in your vehicle. It is a good idea to have a fire extinguisher, and a first aid kit with some basic medical supplies. Also, if you have any medical problems demanding medication, be sure to always keep a large supply on hand—some in your auto and some at home. Sentinel Bear and Crysalis keep a year's supply of their basic medications which they rotate for continual freshness. If you wear glasses, keep an extra pair available.

I feel that people need to learn to share with each other again. This is the purpose of the Bear Tribe and of *Wildfire Magazine* that we publish. We are trying to share our knowledge and resources and create a network with others to do the same. This is very important now because when one area may not be suitable for survival, another will be. When one place may have certain things like foodstuffs, another may have supplies or be able to make shoes, for instance. If these people know each other and can hook up, maybe they can help each other survive. Part of my vision is that people will come together in small communities to survive and they will share their knowledge and abilities and not worry about trying to out do each other. They won't compete over things like who is making more money. I see these different communities working together, too.

Wildfire is called "the Medicine Wheel Network Magazine" because we are attempting to create a network, a sharing between individuals and communities. Up until recently, this sharing has had more to do with knowledge because there are so many people who are not sure what is going on and they want information. But we are working more towards hooking people up with each other, people who have resources and abilities that they wish to share with others, to keep it all going.

With *Wildfire* we are also connecting and setting up land bases across the country. A strong part of my vision is that there will be places where people can go that will help them survive. If people can come together in these places and learn to work with each other and share, then they can get into a better balance and learn to respect the earth and begin to hear her.

For people in the cities, I recommend that you store food and water. Particularly, store food and seasonings that you like to eat, because you can get pretty tired of eating the same bland food for long lengths of time. Things like dried foods, beans, grains, and herbs, are important to have. Keep stored water on hand at all times.

I warned people about doing this in Cincinnati and then they had a major chemical spill and couldn't drink the water. We have to be aware that such accidents are a reality now, and be prepared for them.

SURVIVAL CHECK LIST
Here is a comprehensive survival and wilderness equipment list. This list is extensive. Not all the items may apply to you and your needs. You should remember to rotate your food and water and medication, so it is always fresh. I advise you to keep a supply of vitamins on hand, as many of the storable foods are lacking total nutritional value.

Shelter

Tent or tents depending on
your needs
Sleeping bag for every
member of the family

Extra blankets
Teddybear
Sleeping pads for everyone
Tarps and ground cloth

Food

(Amounts indicate one-year supply for one adult)

300 lbs. of wheat
80 lbs. of powdered milk
150 lbs. of dried beans
(including protein-rich
soybeans)

60 lbs. of honey
50 lbs. of peanut butter
Food for pets

Note: This is your staples list. You should also include canned
goods, freeze-dried food, dried fruit, and any other goodies you are
used to having in your diet. Also, remember to store your food in
moisture-, mouse-, and insect-proof containers.

Water

Store enough water to get you through any foreseeable crisis (you
will need enough for drinking, cooking, and cleaning so figure at
least three to four quarts per family member per day)

Canteens
Spare water containers for
catching and storing rain
water

Water testing kit
A good water-filtering device
Water purification tablets

Kitchen

Manual can opener
Manual grain grinder with a
stone buhr
Camp stove or barbeque pit
Fuel for cooking (charcoal,
charcoal starter, stove fuel)
Pots and pans (camping cook

kits store best, but aren't as
nice to cook on)
Plates and bowls (these
usually come in good
camping cook kits)
Cooking utensils (cook's
knife, spoon, ladle, spatula)

Eating utensils (knives, forks, and spoons)

Matches dipped in wax and stored in waterproof container

Heavy-duty aluminum foil

Biodegradable dish soap

Towels

Bucket and scrub brush

Lighting and Power

Flashlight with spare bulbs and batteries

Candles

Lantern-propane, white gas, or kerosene

Spare propane, white gas (Coleman fuel), or kerosene

Spare wicks and lamp mantles

Gasoline generator

Communication

Portable, solar, or battery operated AM/FM radio

Two-way radio, optional

battery powered (not a citizens band)

Hand-held radios, at least two

Tools

Sturdy, dependable all purpose knife, (keep it sharp and keep it on you)

Sharpening stone

Shovel

Broom

Axe or hatchet

Saw

Hammer

Assorted nails

Assorted screws

File

Wire cutters or pliers

Wrench set

Adjustable wrench

Pipe wrench

Screw drivers (phillips and standard)

200-foot ¼-inch nylon rope

100-foot strong cord

A couple of rolls of duct tape

Coil of bailing wire

Fire extinguisher (A-B-C type)

Tire chains

Sanitation and Medical Supplies

Well-stocked first-aid kit that you know how to use

First-aid book

Snakebite kit

134

Insect repellent
Chapstick
Sunscreen
Mirror
Medication (one year's supply for each family member who is taking medication)
Identification (medical allergies or restrictions)
An extra set of glasses for every family member who wears glasses
Portable toilet (either a chemical toilet or plastic bag type)
Toilet paper
Solar shower

Soap
Premoistened towelettes
Feminine supplies
Infant supplies
Large trash bags (for trash, waste, water protection, and ground cloth)
Powdered chlorinates or lime to add to sewage to deodorize, disinfect, and keep insects away
Toothbrush
Tooth powder or paste (you can use salt and baking soda if you've got it)
Dental floss (this is one of those multi-use items)

Clothing

Several complete changes of clothing, suitable for your area, for every member of the family, stored to be kept dry and safe from moths (Remember that kids are growing and plan for it.)

Warm coats, sweaters, and vests
Rain gear
Sturdy shoes (sneakers or hiking shoes)
Work gloves
Hats and caps
Bandanas and scarves

Hunting, Trapping, and Fishing

Shotgun and/or rifle
Ammunition, at least 200 rounds for each gun (this should be rotated)
Box traps
Fishing poles, hooks, line, lures, and storable bait

Casting net
Bow and arrows (These require special skills, but save ammunition for the guns and do not frighten creatures away from the area.)

Miscellaneous

Compass

Note pad and pencil or pen

Whistle

Money

HELP HEAL THE EARTH

After you have thought about preparing yourself for the earth changes, I strongly suggest you think about ways of lessening their severity by helping to heal the earth now. Since I've suggested you let officials know how you feel, I want to give you specifics on what to do.

Writing letters is an extremely effective means of advocating change in our system of government. Your opinion matters to the politicians in office. Your votes get and keep them in their positions. Utilize your power. Write or call and tell the people who represent you what you think. Here are some tips on letter writing.

1. Keep to one subject as much as possible.
2. Be clear but brief. One page is sufficient.
3. Begin with a statement of purpose, then expand on your views.
4. Although many of the issues you'll write about will be emotional and personal to you, keep your arguments factual so as not to lose the attention of the possibly emotionally detached person receiving the letter.
5. Philosophy seldom sways a politician's views. They want to know how votes will affect the elections. Give them facts, documentation, and illustrations.
6. Explain the situation. They may not be as informed as you think.
7. Include the number (if you know it) and the content matter of a bill that concerns you, as there may be several bills concerned with any one issue.
8. Attitude carries weight. Officials are like most people. A courteous, optimistic letter is more likely to impress them than a defeatest or threatening letter.
9. Check to make sure your name and address are on both the letter and the envelope.
10. If writing any legislator, address them as Honorable on the envelope and inside addresses. Representatives are addressed Mr., Ms., or Mrs. while senators are called "Senator."

11. Be courteous and tactful but remember, you are the boss. Your vote gets these people into office and you pay their salaries. Don't put writing off until tomorrow, or tomorrow might not come.

In appendix B: A Resource Guide for Healing the Earth, you will find suggestions about whom to write to, as well as a list of groups working to make a difference.

FEEL AND CHANGE

The problem of people's ability to think and not feel is the crux of much of the dilemma upon our Earth Mother today. If people would learn to feel the life force and the energies of our planet, they would be better able to understand why we must take better care of the earth and our environment.

I keep searching for ways in which people can experience their own feelings. This is my first action as a teacher. I feel this is the bottom line in spirituality. Learning how to feel things is hard, mainly because of the whole conditioning that society has put on you to make you think instead of feel. People are taught to accept nature as something you walk over and just take from. To native people, all parts of the creation are living intelligent beings with feelings of their own.

Peter Tomkins wrote a book a while back called *The Secret Life of Plants.* He acknowledges in it that all plants have power, consciousness, and feeling. Scientists have hooked sensory machines up to plants which went haywire when the plants were ripped from the ground. They did similar tests with fertilized eggs. They placed them on a conveyor belt, then dropped one randomly chosen egg, into scalding, hot water. The rest of the eggs responded hysterically, which was recorded scientifically with testing devices.

These, and similar experiments, show even nonfeeling thinkers that everything is alive. The planet itself is a living being. I tell people the planet is like a great big shaggy dog and we are just fleas. When the fleas get out of control, the dog freaks out and starts shaking them off.

Which brings me to the threat of nuclear war. A nuclear war could be the biggest flea bath possible, and it would be by our own hand.

The United States is the only country that has ever used nuclear weapons on our fellow human beings. We still seem to be naive and emotionally immature about the hazards, effects, and finality of these weapons. According to the book *Last Aid*, prepared by International Physicians for the Prevention of Nuclear War, statistics show that over 78 million people have been killed in conventional warfare since the 1900. This, as sad as it is, is nothing compared to what would happen in a nuclear war. We could be looking at hundreds of millions of deaths and possibly no survivors at all. Whole cultures would be destroyed. Survivors would have to live in poisoned lands. It has been said that those who survive will envy the dead.

In late 1987 the United States and Russia had about 50,000 nuclear warheads. This equals three tons of TNT for every man, woman, and child on our planet, a total of 15 billion tons of TNT. The power to destroy with this is equivalent to 1,250,000 Hiroshima bombs. But still, in 1989 the Pentagon asked for $300 billion to spend in one year on the military. Also worth noting is that the fanciful Strategic Defense initiative, the so-called Star Wars antimissile scheme, carries a price tag of $3 trillion. To give you an idea of what a trillion dollars can represent let me share some statistics. If you were to count a trillion one-dollar bills, one per second, twenty-four hours a day, it would take thirty-two years. Or, with $1 trillion, you could buy a $100,000 house for every family in Kansas, Missouri, Nebraska, Oklahoma, and Iowa. Then you could put a $10,000 car in every garage of each of those houses. There would be enough left to build libraries and hospitals in 250 cities at the cost of $10 million per city. Then you could build 500 schools for 500 communities at $10 million for each community. And, there would still be enough left to put in the bank and, from the interest alone, pay 10,000 nurses and teachers, plus give a $5000 bonus to every family in the aforementioned states.

FINDING THE HUNDREDTH MONKEY
Often, upon hearing such statistics, there is an overwhelming feeling of helplessness. People ask, "What can I do about it?" Keep in mind that a number of times in the course of the history of the United States grass roots public opinion and action has had a profound effect upon public policy. The peace movement during the Vietnam War and the human rights movement in the sixties are just

two of many dramatic examples. The potential impact of awareness and communication is illustrated by the research that has become known as the "100th-Monkey-Syndrome," written about by Ken Keyes, Jr.

This is the story of when, starting with one monkey, a crucial number of monkeys on some islands in the Pacific began to wash their food source in a new way. Not knowing the exact amount, we will say that when the 100th monkey washed his food in this way, the practice was picked up by the whole colony of monkeys although some were separated from the main group by the ocean. This 100th monkey theory implies that when a certain critical number of a group achieves an awareness, this new awareness may be communicated among them from mind to mind. Although the exact number may vary, there is a point at which if only one more person tunes in to a new awareness, a field is strengthened so that this awareness is picked up by everyone—you could be the 100th monkey. Your awareness is essential in preventing further damage to the earth. Your communication with someone about the survival of the Earth Mother may be the added conscious energy that can sway the healing of our planet.

People really are beginning to see that the way the planet is being treated does not work. This is why people are drawn toward the native teachings and the old ways. Now, with the future in such a delicate balance, people are saying, "Hey, maybe these folks have an answer."

Life is very interesting. Now, I have one apprentice who is an IBM executive. He has started meditation programs in his office for his employees. He has gotten his managers and sales reps smudging themselves and the office daily. There are also doctors, other business executives, scientists, lawyers, psychiatrists, and even an ex-FBI man who have come to my workshops.

Some of these are people who characteristically tend to look at life rather dogmatically, as if there is only one point of view to life, and that's that. This is changing. People are beginning to open up, to see things in new and alternative ways. They are letting go of their tunnel vision. This is going to make the difference. It's tunnel vision that has gotten us into trouble with everything in the universe. Somehow we are going to have to be willing to acknowledge our own stupidity and open up to other ways of looking at things.

At an apprentice program of mine, someone came across a road-kill deer that was still fresh and edible with the skin in good shape. So I had all the new students help me skin it. There they were, mostly city dwellers in this particular program, and even one man who was a nuclear physicist skinning this deer. We were talking about how delicious the venison, the nice steaks, and stew meat would be, and how grateful we were that the deer gifted itself to us and how we would honor the skin by using it in a good way.

Then we started talking about the earth changes. One of the people asked me if I thought there was hope for the world and our people. I said, "Oh yes, there's a lot of hope for the world when I can have a nuclear physicist here skinning a road-kill deer."

We need to look at all these things at this time. We human beings should take it upon ourselves, as a personal responsibility, to do our best to make the necessary corrections to the way we relate to the earth by conserving the environment and natural resources in a real way. Such responsibility has to become a spiritual way with us. We must practice responsibility and conservation everyday, and teach our young people to do the same so that this good way will be passed on and there will be future generations.

Appendix A:
A Resource Guide to
Healing Places, Associations,
and People

This section of the resource guide lists the addresses of places where you can go to experience healing of various types, and the addresses of associations which can help you find local people who practice their particular form of healing. This is not a comprehensive list. It only contains some of the places we have personally experienced in some way or another.

If a place offers a variety of healing methods or other services, or if I did not describe their methods in chapter 10, I have supplied short descriptions of the work they do. Some listings I have prefaced with the subject area in parenthesis, since I think they will be easier to find under the subject.

Abode of the Message. The Abode was founded by Pir Vilayat Inayat Khan to further the work of the Sufi Order and provide a community atmosphere in which people can strive to bring spirituality into their everyday lives. The community offers retreats and conference facilities. For more information, contact: Abode of The Message, R D 1, Box 1030 D, New Lebanon, NY 12125 (518)794-8090.

Acupressure Institute, 1533 Shattuck Ave., Berkley, CA 94709. (415)845-1059.

American Center for Alexander Technique, 142 West End Ave., New York, NY 10023.

American College of Orgonomy, P.O. Box 490, Princeton, NJ 08542. (201)821-1144. Publishes the *Journal of Orgonomy*.

American Osteopathic Association, 142 East Ontario St., Chicago, IL 60611. (312)280-5800.

Ananda Cooperative Village. A large community and retreat center founded upon the teachings of Swami Kriyananda. For more information contact: Ananda Cooperative Village, 14618 Tyler Foot Rd., Nevada City, CA 95959. (916)292-3494.

Arica. The Arica School is a school for consciousness developed by Oscar Ichazo to meet the requirements of the times in which we live. The Arica theory and method of spiritual work are directed toward the enlightenment and benefit of all humanity. For more information contact: Arica, 150 Fifth Ave., Suite 912, New York City, NY 10011.

Association for Holistic Health. Publishes a newsletter and the National Directory of Holistic Health Practitioners. For more information contact: Association for Holistic Health, P.O. Box 9532, San Diego, CA 92109. (619)275-2694.

Association of Holistic Practitioners, Department CC, P.O. Box 19426, Pittsburg, PA 15213. (412)412-2057.

Association for Research and Enlightenment (A.R.E.). This is a living network of people who are finding a deeper meaning in life through the psychic work of Edgar Cayce. For more information write: A.R.E., Inc., P.O. Box 595, Virginia Beach, VA 23451. (804)428-3588.

The Ayurvedic Center, 17308 Sunset Blvd., Pacific Palisades, CA 90272. (213)454-5531

The Dr. Edward Bach Healing Center, Mount Vernon, Sotwell, Wallingford, Oxon, England.

The Bear Tribe. The Bear Tribe is the community I helped found. Our main base is located on Vision Mountain near Spokane, Washington. There we have Apprentice programs, Vision Quests, Permaculture courses, and other activities. The Bear Tribe also has affiliates around the country and in Europe who give workshops and teach about earth awareness and earth healing. For more information, contact: The Bear Tribe, P.O. Box 9167, Spokane, WA 99209-9167, (509)326-6561.

Biofeedback Institute of Los Angeles, 6399 Wilshire Blvd., No. 900, Los Angeles, CA 90048. (213)933-9451.

Chinook Learning Center. Chinook offers workshops, conferences, and journeys based upon a hopeful vision of human life and the future of the earth. For more information, contact: Chinook Learning Center, 4769 E. Highway 525, Clinton, WA 98236. (206)321-1884.

California Institute of Transpersonal Psychology, 250 Oak Grove, Menlo Park, CA 94025. (415)326-1960.

Colorado Outward Bound School (COBS). For over twenty-five years COBS has broadened participants' physical, mental, social, and academic horizons. Through a unique combination of outdoor challenge, skills training, and adventure, a COBS course enhances intellectual curiosity, responsibility, initiative, and compassion for others. A manageable series of physical and mental challenges help build confidence and draw out the best in people. For more information, contact: Colorado Outward Bound School, 945 Pennsylvania St., Denver, CO 80203-3198, (303)837-0880.

The Dance of the Deer Foundation. Founded by Brant Secunda in 1980, this group offers workshops in Huichol Indian Shamanism throughout the world. The Foundation also sponsors pilgrimages to special places of power as a means for each individual to create and maintain a beautiful and powerful relationship with the natural world.

Ceremony and sacred dance, practices of health and shamanic healing, prayer circles, dream-work, and explorations of art and cosmology are techniques of Huichol Shamanism, taught in order to obtain life force for our own well-being and that of all planetary life. Weekend, weeklong, or long-term advanced programs are offered. Special programs are offered with Don Jose Matsuwa, the renowned Huichol Shaman. For more information write: Dance of the Deer Foundation, Center for Shamanic Studies, P.O. Box 699 Soquel, CA 95073. (408)475-9560.

The Earthstone Institute. This group will send you more information about getting a Medicine Wheel consultation or an Earthstone Reading. For more information, contact: The Earthstone Institute, P.O. Box 9167, Spokane, WA 99209. (509)326-6561.

The Esalen Institute. A center at which to explore trends in education, religion, philosophy, and the physical and behavioral sciences which emphasize the potentialities and the value of human existence. Its activities consist of seminars and workshops, residential programs, consulting, and research. Beautiful hot tubs overlook the ocean. Esalen offers a large spectrum of highly acclaimed workshops and seminars on many topics of current interest. For more information, contact: Esalen Institute, Big Sur, CA 93920. (408)667-3000.

The Feathered Pipe Ranch Foundation. A beautiful ranch nestled in the Montana Rockies, just a few miles from the Continental Divide. It is named after the feathered pipe—the sacred pipe which native Americans have long used in ceremonies to connect all beings within the circle of life. Feathered Pipe Ranch offers programs that help humans know their inherent wholeness and interconnectedness with all of life. Their many programs have included workshops by Dr. Bernard Jensen on the course of life, Brant Secunda on shamanism, Lilias Folan on yoga, and much more. For more information contact: The Feathered Pipe Ranch, Box 1682, Helena, MT 59624. (406)442-8196.

The Flower Essence Society, P.O. Box 459, Nevada City, CA 95959.

The Feldenhrais Guild Directory, P.O. Box 111454, Main Office, San Francisco, CA 94101

Fox Valley Gestalt Center, 130 West State St., Geneva, IL 60134. (312)232-1223.

The Gestalt Directory, P.O. Box 490, Highland, NY 12528.

Glen Ivy Hot Springs. A natural Californian hot springs spa in the Mediterranean style. A continuous flow of skin-soothing, mineral-rich hot water fills thirteen pools, baths, and spas in varying temperatures, up to 104 degrees. They have spas, pools, mineral baths, saunas, mud baths, and aquaexercise classes. The staff provides the latest in Swedish, Shiatsu and Hydrotherapy massages, European facials, herbal wraps, and skin glow treatments. Open daily from 10:00 AM to 6:00 PM For more information contact: Glen Ivy Hot Springs, 25000 Glen Ivy Rd., Corona, CA 91719. (714)737-4723.

Harbin Hot Springs. A New Age retreat and teaching center, located two hours north of the San Francisco Bay Area. There you can relax and enjoy mineral water, hot, warm and cold pools, and sauna. You can explore 1,600 acres of woods, streams, and meadows. A qualified massage staff is available. For more information write: Harbin Hot Springs, P.O. Box 782, Middletown, CA 95461. (800)622-2477.

Heartwood Institute. Created by individuals who are guided to the calling of natural healing through nurturing touch, they are committed to a new model of health which is person-centered rather than disease-centered, and to competence and professionalism in preventive health care. They have compassion for the human condition, and look toward the person and the challenges of living for an understanding of disease and health. They assist the person in taking responsibility for his own health and life. They provide resources for attaining higher physical, psychological, and spiritual well-being, accomplished through programs of study, workshops, and wellness retreats offered to both professionals and the general public. For more information contact: Heartwood Institute, 220 Harmony lane, Garberville, CA 95440 (707)923-2021

(Herbology) California School of Herbal Studies. Founded by Rosemary Gladstar, the school provides both residential and correspondence herbal courses, as well as conferences and sacred journeys. For more information contact: California School of Herbal Studies, P.O. Box 39, Forestville, CA 95436.

(Herbology) The Spirit and Essence of Herbs. A seven month apprenticeship program, one weekend per month, with Rosemary Gladstar, one of the country's leading herbalists. For more information contact: Rosemary Gladstar, P.O. Box 420, E. Barre, VT 05649.

(Herbology) Willow Rain Herb Farm. Willow Rain grows and wildcrafts herbs, and prepares them in a sacred manner. Pat Tuholske is an apprentice to Sun Bear and a specialist in the herbs of the Medicine Wheel. For more information, contact: Willow Rain Herb Farm, P.O. Box 15, Grubville, MO 63041. Attn: Pat Tuholske.

Hippocrates World Health Institute. Information about diet, fasting and wheat grass. For more information, contact: Hippocrates World Health Institute, 25 Exeter St., Boston. MA 02116.

Homeopathic Educational Services. They have a directory of homeopaths in the United States, and distribute books, tapes and medicine kits. For more information, contact: Homeopathic Educational Services, 21224 Kittredge St., Berkley, CA 94704.

Images in Motion. Workshops in dance for people with disabilities. Founder/Director, Patricia Fulton, M.A., presents workshops nationwide for universities, professional organizations, public schools, and other agencies. Integrating theory with practical application, Patricia guides participants through a process which will enable them to facilitate movement and dance with persons who have disabilities and/or special needs. Educational videos are available. There are ongoing classes in Boulder. For more information, write: Images In Motion, 1085 14th St., Boulder, CO 80302. (303)444-7926.

International Institute for Bioenergetic Analysis, 144 E. 36 St., 1A, New York, NY 10016.

Institute for Creative Aging. This organization provides services which enable families to assist their aging relatives. They deal with such issues as: planning for the future, loss, grief, guilt, financial planning, legal issues, counseling, community resource information, social services, and mental health. This organization is building a bridge of communication between generations. For more information, write: Institute for Creative Aging, P.O. Box 3725, Littleton, CO 80161. (303)795-9682.

Institute of Psycho-Structural Balancing (IPSB). Founded in 1977, IPSB has earned the reputation of being innovative and devoted to the art and science of contemporary bodywork and massage. For more information, contact: Institute of Psycho-Structural Balancing, 4502 Cass St., San Diego, CA 92109. (619)272-4142.

Joy Lake Mountain Seminar Center. Joy Lake is in the heart of the eastern Sierras, located adjacent to the Toiyabe National Forest and to the 1,200 acres of the Whittell Audubon Society. Many of their workshops are held in natural surroundings. The wilderness setting provides the individual with an opportunity for introspection in a relaxed environment. Joy Lake provides a vast variety of progressive workshops, including several by me each year. Other workshops explore herbology, sufism, relationship, sound and vibration, Hatha yoga, Buddhism, stone therapy, and more. For more information, contact: Joy Lake Mountain Seminar Center, P.O. Box. 1328, Reno, NV 89504. (702)323-0378.

C. G. Jung Foundation for Analytical Psychology. This foundation is based upon the work of Carl Jung, a psychoanalyst whose theories form part of the foundation for both the humanistic and transpersonal psychology movements. For more information, contact: C. G. Jung Foundation for Analytical Psychology, 28 East 39th St., New York, NY 10016. (212)697-6430.

Kripalu Center for Holistic Health, P.O. Box 120, Summit Station, PA 17979.

(Macrobiotics) The Kushi Foundation, P.O. Box 1100, Brookline Village, MA 02147. (617)738-0045.

(Macrobiotics) The Kushi Institute. Provides a comprehensive macrobiotic education. For more information contact: The Kushi Institute, P.O. Box 7, Becket, MA 01223. (413)623-5712.

(Men) A Man's Weekend. Experience the teachings and concepts of the poet Robert Bly, getting back to the deep-rootedness of your maleness through story, fables, legends, and the tribal experience. Particular emphasis is placed on the bonding, or lack thereof with one's father, and the effects this has had upon relating in the world and with those you love. For more information write: Ed Block-Farrington, M.A., and Randy Berlin, Ph.D. 529 Central Ave., Pacific Grove, CA 93950. (408)372-2711 or (408)375-5410.

(Men) Austin Men's Center, 4204 Ave. F, Austin, TX 78751. (512)453-8192.

(Men) Men Awakening. Participating in this group is an invitation to explore the depths of masculinity in a supportive circle of men. At various times during the year council is held on Maui where sacred space is created for owning one's manhood. The facilitators of these groups are also available for consultation and workshops in other states. For more information write: David Grace-Charry and Allen Jay White, Star Route 1, Box 161 Haiku, Maui, HI 96708. (808)572-9300.

(Men) Teaching Men in the Ways Men Learn Best. The purpose of this organization is to coach men in the skills which enable them to grapple successfully with challenges caused by changing male roles, working conditions, cultural stereotypes, and social expectations. The organization conducts local and international public and in-house educational events about communication, collaboration, intimacy, and commitment between men and women. They consult with organizations about gender issues in the workplace, design study materials for men, and provide briefings for women about men's attitudes, behavior, and language. For more information write: Hidden Valley Center For Men, P.O. Box 392, Soquel, CA 95073. (408)476-4167.

(Men) Men's Resource Center, 3534 Southeast Main Street, Portland, OR 97214. (503)235-3433.

Mount Madonna Center. The Mount Madonna Center for the Creative Arts and Sciences is a community designed to nurture the creative arts and health sciences within a context of spiritual growth. The Center is inspired by Baba Hari Dass and is sponsored by the Hanuman Fellowship, a group whose talents and interests are unified by the common practice of yoga. For more information contact: Mount Madonna Center, 445 Summit Road, Watsonville, CA 95076.

Murrieta Hot Springs Resort & Health Spa. Feeling good about ourselves is vital to every aspect of life. When stressed, we seek calm and healing. When relationships are in doubt, we want clarity, direction, and renewed self-esteem. When the body slows or health falters, we need rebuilding and energizing. Murrieta has programs that give personal attention to meeting these and other real needs, producing a sense of well-being and confidence that can enable you to maintain your own balance in life. Their supportive teaching staff helps you to have fun while you revitalize your health. The programs blend wellness activities for both body and mind, resulting in high levels of relaxation. For more information contact: Murrieta Hot Springs Resort & Health Spa, 39405 Murrieta Hot Springs Rd., Murrieta, CA 92362. Inside California: (800)458-4393, Outside California: (800)322-4542.

Naropa Institute. Provides programs on both the undergraduate and graduate level in the arts and humanities based upon the principles of contemplative education. For more information contact: Naropa Institute, 2130 Arabahoe Ave., Boulder, CO 80302.

National Iridology Research Association. This association was founded for the purpose of increasing and sharing knowledge concerning the art and science of iridology. For more information write: National Iridology Research Association, P.O. Box 5277-C, Santa Fe, NM 87502. (505)983-6193.

National New Age Yellow Pages. A United States guide to conscious-raising resources. For more information write: NNAYP, P.O. Box 5491-C, Fullerton, CA 92635.

New Jersey School of Massage, 3699 Route 46, E. Parsipanny, NJ 07054. (201)263-2292.

New Mexico Academy of Massage and Advanced Healing Arts, P.O. Box 932, Santa Fe, NM 87504. (505)982-6271.

New Mexico School of Natural Therapeutics, 106 Girad S.E., Suite 107, Albuquerque, NM 87106. (505)286-6870.

Ojai Foundation. A small community, Ojai is also a retreat and educational center that brings together teachers from different spiritual traditions. For more information contact: Ojai Foundation, P.O. Box 1620, Ojai, CA 93023. (805)646-8343.

Omega Institute. Omega is a comprehensive holistic retreat center sponsoring a wide variety of programs. For more information contact: Omega Institute, Box 571 A, Lebanon Springs, NY 12114.

Ortho-Bionomy International, Inc., 12115 Magnolia Blvd. #152, N. Hollywood, CA 91607.

Peetham: A Center for Well-Being. The Peetham sponsors a variety of programs on holistic living. For more information contact: Peetham: A Center for Well-Being, R.D. 8, Box 8116, Stroudsberg, PA 18360. (717)629-0481.

(Permaculture) Abundant Life Seed Foundation, Abundant Life provides both heirloom and traditional seeds. For more information, contact: Abundant Life Seed Foundation, P.O. Box, 772, Port Townsend, WA 98368.

(Permaculture) Bear Creek Nursery. Bear Creek provides hardy fruit and nut trees, and shrubs. For more information contact: Bear Creek Nursery, P.O. Box 411, Northport, WA 99157.

(Permaculture) The International Green Front Report. There is a seven-dollar charge for this report, which tells you everything you want to know (and some things you probably will wish you didn't know) about the state of the earth. For more information contact: The International Green Front Report, Michael Pilarski, Director, Friends of the Trees, P.O. Box 1466, Chelan, WA 98816.

(Permaculture) T.I.P.S.Y. This is a yearly periodic resource manual about plants, species, aquaculture, and more. For more information contact: T.I.P.S.Y. The International Permaculture Species Yearbook, P.O. Box 202, Orange, MA 01364.

(Permaculture) Seed Saver Exchange, Kent Wheatly, Director, RR 3, Box 239, Decorah, IA 52101.

Polarity Therapy Center of San Francisco, 409-A Lawton St. San Francisco, CA 94122.

The Pritikin Longevity Center. This center is doing work with and research in cardiovascular diseases, high blood pressure, diabetes, and other illnesses. Maximum emphasis is put on reduction of fat and cholesterol intake through a low-fat diet of unrefined foods and fiber-rich carbohydrates. Research has shown that for many, this diet has been excellent for combating such diseases as large bowel cancer, gallstones, varicose veins, hemorrhoids, diverticular disease of the colon, appendicitis, hiatal hernia, high blood pressure, heart disease, and diabetes. Americans have a fifty-fifty chance of dying of a stroke or heart disease before their time. This diet, combined with proper exercise, has helped many live longer fuller lives. For more information contact: The Pritikin Longevity Center, 1910 Ocean Front Walk, Santa Monica, CA 90405. (213)450-5433. (For other locations in other states call or write this address).

(Reflexology) New York School for Shiatsu and Reflexology, 149 E. 81st St., New York, NY 10028. (212)472-2242.

(Reflexology) Stirling Enterprises, P.O. Box 216, Cottage Grove, OR 97424, (503)942-4622.

(Reflexology) Reflexology/Ministry of Healing, 3828 Kramer St., Harrisburg, PA 17109.

(Reflexology) Reflexology Workshop, 1533 Shattuck, Berkley, CA 94709

Reevaluation Counselling, 719 Second Ave. North, Seattle, WA 98109.

(Reiki) American International Reiki Association, P.O. Box 86038, St. Petersburg, FL 33738. (813)360-7154

(Reiki) Renaissance, 2147 Oakland Dr., Kalamazoo, MI 49008. (616)385-2119.

Rivendell Holistic Retreat. This retreat provides rebirthing, group rebirths and seminars, yoga and meditation classes, polarity and Reiki massage by appointment, psychotherapy, and psychic counselling. They provide a secluded setting in the woods, with deck and a hot tub. For more information write: Rivendell Holistic Retreat, 3 Old Mill Road, Weston, CT 06883. (203)227-3559.

The Rolf Institute, P.O. Box 1868, Boulder CO. 80306. (303)449-5903.

Roots & Wings. This is a sensitive multimethod process developed by Punja Tobey which includes gestalt, visualizations, meditation, encounter, past-life regressions, and Bach-Flower Remedies. For more information write: Roots & Wings, Punja

Tobey, 153-Z Zena Highwoods Road, Kingston, NY 12401. (914)679-5580.

The Santa Barbara College of Oriental Medicine, 1919 State Street Suite 204, Santa Barbara, CA 93101. (805)682-9594.

Shakti Gawain Workshops. Shakti Gawain, author of *Creative Visualization*, has created the Shakti Center in Marin County, California, where she and her staff conduct ongoing classes and weekend workshops. The emphasis is on communication, healing old beliefs and emotional patterns, establishing intimacy in one's life, and exploring new ways of expressing oneself creatively. For more information write: Shakti Center, P.O. Box 377, Mill Valley, CA 94942. (415)927-2277.

The Source of Life Enrichment Center, 2726 Ellendale St., St. Louis, MO 63143. (314)644-0641.

Sun Ray Meditation Society. Disseminates information about the work of Dhyani Ywahoo. For more information write: Sun Ray Meditation Society, The Peacekeeper Mission, RD1, Box 87, Huntington, VT 05462.

(Tai Chi) Pacific School of Tai Chi, P.O. Box 8254, La Jolla, CA 92038. (619)259-1396.

Touch for Health Foundation, 1174 North Lake Ave., Pasadena, CA 91104

(Vision Quest) The School of Lost Borders. The school, founded by Steven Foster and Meredith Little, authors of *The Book Of The Vision Quest*, teaches vision quest guides. At the same address is Rites of Passage Press which publishes books about the Vision Quest. For more information write: The School of Lost Borders, P.O. Box 55, Big Pine, CA 93513

The Voice Workshop. This workshop teaches that one's voice is a tool for healing. It explores breathing, posture, relaxation, resonance, vowels, and physiology, as well as chakras, colors, and hands-on healing. For more information write: The Voice Workshop, 317 West 3rd Street #3B, New York, NY 10025, Attn: John Eppler. (212)799-0407 or (212)662-9338.

Water Filters, Joseph Mulligan, 11540 Tamiami Trail, E. Naples, FL 33962.

(Women) National Women's Health Network, 2025 First Street N.W., Suite 105, Washington DC 20006.

(Women) Women's Information Exchange, 1195 Valencia Street, San Francisco, CA 94110.

(Women) **Women's International Network,** 187 Grant St., Lexington, MA 02173. (617)862-9431.

Woman's Referral Service, P.O. Box 3093, Van Nuys, CA 91407. (818)995-6646

HEALING PEOPLE

I know many healers. Listing them all would take a separate book. The people mentioned here are some of my apprentices, people who have been to our Medicine Wheel Gatherings to teach, and a few healing friends. It is the Bear Tribe's policy not to give out addresses for medicine people unless they have a public foundation and ask that we let people know where to contact them. So you won't find many addresses here. If you really need to contact someone on this list, send the Bear Tribe your letter to the person (with the proper postage on it) and a note requesting that they forward it.

Amylee. Hawk Hollow, Tippecanoe, Ohio 44699-9612. Amylee is born of a lineage of Iroquois medicine way women and is the last of that lineage. She is an initiate, not yet a medicine woman. She travels across Mother Earth teaching the ways of her people, about women and their sacred cycles, and about crystals and other members of the mineral kingdom. She also is an accomplished craftswoman and counselor.

Gray Antelope. This Tewa Pueblo medicine man is a chanter, dancer, and a healer. He and his Humbios Clan Dancers have danced at many Medicine Wheel Gatherings.

Dr. Frans Bakker. The Director of the Radiant Life Clinic in California. He is a teacher of radical spiritual healing and a specialist on rejuvenation health techniques.

Elke Baumgarten. Berg en Dalseweg 292, 6522 CN Nijmegen, Holland. Elke is the Bear Tribe's regional coordinator for Holland, and a long-time apprentice to Sun Bear. She teaches about earth awareness.

Bear Heart. A Muskogee tribal medicine chief and respected leader of the native American Church. He has sundanced with both the northern and southern Cheyenne people.

Jones Benally Family. Native American champion dancers and entertainers, adhering to Navajo tradition and culture. They have danced at Medicine Wheel Gatherings.

Wallace Black Elk. He has trained since childhood in the ways of the Earth People to become a Lakota holy man. Spirit has chosen Wallace Black Elk as a spiritual guide for all of the people. His grandfather Black Elk, shared his vision with the world in the book *Black Elk Speaks.*

Judith Trustone Brigham. The ReVitalization Centers, Box 313, Upper Darby, PA 19082 (215)352-7017. Judith Trustone, an apprentice to Sun Bear, is the executive director of the ReVitalization Centers in the Philadelphia area where holistic counseling, education, and bodywork is provided. A few of the topics Judith teaches about are crystals, relationships, stress management, Earth Encounters, and the native American approach to wellness. She is also a Medicine Wheel Consultant. With Margie White and Dixie Carlson she is the Pennsylvania and New Jersey area regional coordinator for the Bear Tribe.

Tom Brown, Jr. He studied wilderness survival and nature appreciation under the Apache medicine man Stalking Wolf. He is the author of several books on tracking and survival. He is one of the foremost survival instructors and trackers in the world.

Betsy Browne. 77 Laurel Lane, Lunenberg, MA 01462. A networker, teacher, and Bear Tribe New England area coordinator.

Page Bryant-Guynup. An internationally known psychic, lecturer, author, and radio personality. For the past seventeen years, she has been receiving teachings from an interdimensional being known as Albion. Page is the author of *Terravision* (Spring, 1990 publication), *The Earth Changes Survival Handbook, Crystals and Their Use,* and *The Magic of Minerals.* All are available from The Network for Cooperative Education, 130 Pinto Lane, Sedona, AZ 86336.

Tess Carbajal. She has her own practice using holistic therapies. She received her training from the International Academy of Clinical Acupuncture in Kansas City. For the past eight years, she has been learning to tune into the native American aspect of herself, which has included a study of crystals.

Dixie Carlson. P.O. Box 99,Orangeville, PA 17859. A networker and teacher of Earth Encounter workshops. She is a Bear Tribe Regional Coordinator for the Pennsylvania and New Jersey area.

Norma Cordell (Eagle Morning Star). The director of the Eugene Center of Healing Arts in Oregon. She is a spiritualist, a healer, and the author of *Earth Dance*. She was trained by a Nez Perce shaman.

Becca and Jac Costello. Associated with Light in Motion Crystals, P.O. Box 876, Girdwood, AK 99587.

Lynne Crow. A psychic, a visionary, and a teacher. She helps North Americans to become at home spiritually.

Elisabeth Rhiannon Davis. She acts as the executive director for the Bear Tribe and also teaches apprentice, Vision Quest, and earth awareness programs. She can be contacted through The Bear Tribe, P.O. Box 9167, Spokane, WA 99209-9167.

Joann Davis. A psychotherapist, and an apprentice to Sun Bear. Contact through the Sacred Tree Foundation, 300 Ozark Trail # 102, Ellisville, MO 63011.

Dr. James Demeo. P.O. Box 1395, El Cerrito, CA 94530. He has been researching the topic of the life energy, and specifically the works of Wilhelm Reich for the last fifteen years. His work on the geography of behavior, orgone biophysics, and experimental cloudbusting have been presented at professional meetings, and have been published in various magazines and compendiums.

Dr. James Duke. Considered to be a key figure in the worldwide "herbal renaissance." As a collaborator with the Smithsonian Institute, he has lectured and taught there with an emphasis on neotropical, enthnobiological, and folk medicine.

Vicki Lynn Elliott. 810 Basin Rd., Apt. J2, New Castle, DE 19720. The Bear Tribe Regional Coordinator for Delaware.

Pat Embers. 733 Galaxy, Manhattan, KS 66502. An occupational therapist and Bear Tribe networker.

Oh Shinnah Fastwolf. Dedicated to the healing of the Earth Mother, she is an eclectic person whose teachings come from various ancient traditions.

Lilias Folan. America's best known yoga teacher. Millions of people watch her nationally syndicated television series, "Lilias, Yoga and You," read her many books, and listen to her tapes. No mountaintop mystic, her concerns are very much in the here and now.

Steven Foster and Meredith Little. P.O. Box 55, Big Pine, CA 93513. Coauthors of *The Book of the Vision Quest* and *The Roaring* *of the Sacred River.* They are founders and former codirectors of Rites of Passage, a teaching organization which guides people along the medicine path. They currently direct The School of Lost Borders.

Jan Fowler. Rt. 1, Box 86, Madison, VA 22727. A member of the center management team at Seven Oaks Community, she teaches wilderness and outdoor skills.

Sunshine Garner. A registered nurse and a Bear Tribe networker, she teaches Earth Encounters and does Medicine Wheel Consultations. Contact her through the Earthstone Institute, P.O. Box 9167, Spokane, WA 99209-9167.

Peter Grebot. 4 Warren Lane, Dartington Estates, Totnes, Devon TQ9, England. The Bear Tribe Regional Coordinator for the Devon, England area.

Rosemary Gladstar. P.O. Box 420, E. Barre, VT 05649. A teacher, herbalist, and the founder and former director of the California School of Herbal Studies, she currently teaches an apprenticeship program.

Carol Glover. 732 ½ Don Diego, Santa Fe, NM 87501. Carol is a shamanic healer. In an altered state, she senses energy patterns and identifies problem areas with guidance from the higher self and spiritual teachers. Using a variety of powerful earth tools, she can remove blocks, change patterns, and affect healing on all levels.

Carol and Phil Grigg. 907 N.E. 73rd, Seattle, WA 98115. The Bear Tribe Regional Coordinators for the Western Washington area. Carol teaches Earth Awareness workshops.

Scott Guynup. 130 Pinto Lane, Sedona, AZ 86336. A well-known New Age and psychic artist, Scott also works with the Network for Cooperative Education.

Joan Halifax. The author of *Shaman: The Wounded Healer,* and *Shamanic Voices,* she is also the Director of the Ojai Foundation in Ojai, California.

Hawk Little John. He is of Cherokee descent, a teacher, and a healer. He farms, and lectures about the traditional native ways of healing.

Simon Henderson-Corn Man. An ecological environmentalist and permaculture designer, he is the feature writer of "Simon's Spiral" for *Wildfire* magazine as well as Master Gardener/Director for permaculture courses and self-reliance intensives at the Buffalo Hunt Garden at the Bear Tribe in Spokane. Simon is also founder of an ethnobotanical seed company, The Buffalo Hunt Seed Co. Seeds, sage, and other herbs are available. For information contact: Buffalo Hunt Seed Co., PO Box 9167, Spokane, WA 99209, (509)326-6561.

Charles Hiatt. A physician and one of my apprentices, he practices near St. Louis.

Walt Hoesel. 11925 325th, Duvall, WA 98019. A high school teacher, and apprentice who works with the Bear Tribe as a networker, teacher, and vision quest guide.

Phyllis Hogan. The founder of the Arizona Ethnobotanical Research Association, she has spent the last few decades studying with native American elders and respected Navajo herbalist Sam Boon, Sr.

Auntie Lani Kalama. One of the few true hula resources left in the Hawaiian islands. It is a rare privilege to learn Hula from Auntie Lani as she no longer teaches formal classes.

Karen Kelley. Director of The Sacred Tree Foundation, she is a chiropractor, holistic healer, facilitator of workshops including Earth Awareness workshops, and an apprentice to Sun Bear. This high powered woman is the coordinator of a variety of native American and holistic health workshops and events. Karen is the Bear Tribe Regional Coordinator for Missouri, Iowa, Arkansas, and Louisiana. For more information and brochures contact: Karen Kelley, 300 Ozark Trail # 102, Ellisville, MO 63011. (314)227-0760.

Elizabeth Kubler-Ross. The author of *Death and Dying* and *Living With Death And Dying*, Elizabeth is the director of Shanti Nilaya in Virginia. She is a world renouned teacher and lecturer, and a founding member of the American Holistic Medical Association.

Winona Laduke. She is Sun Bear's daughter, the former director of the Circle of Life Survival School on the White Earth Reservation in Minnesota. She also is an internationally known antinuclear activist, and a recipient of the first Reebok Human-Rights award.

Mary Ann Leberg. She teaches Earth Awareness workshops and does Medicine Wheel consultations. She can be contacted at: 2919 E. Harrison, Seattle, WA 98112.

Anita Maloney. 2615 Tyson, Tampa, FL 33611. She owns a crystal business and is a crystal practitioner.

Manitonquat (Medicine Story). The founder of the Mettanokit community and Keeper of the Lore of the Wampanoag people. He is the director of "Another Place" in New Hampshire and author of the book, *Return To Creation.*

Brigitta Marsen. Goethestrasse 20, 1000 Berlin 37, West Germany. She is a psychotherapist and the Bear Tribe Regional Coordinator for Berlin, Germany.

Brooke Medicine Eagle. P.O. Box 121, Ovando, MT 59854. The great-great-grandniece of Chief Joseph, the Nez Perce holy man and leader. She is trained in the traditions of her people and in western psychology and body work. She has lectured around the world.

Blair Moffett. P.O. Box 366, Chino Valley, AZ 86323. The Bear Tribe Regional Coordinator for the New Mexico, Arizona area.

Jane Montgomery. One of the most highly recommended masseuses this side of Tibet. If you are anywhere near San Francisco, look her up. For more information contact: Jane Montgomery, 138 Alpine Terrace, San Francisco, CA 94117, (415)621-2024.

David Moore. County Road 33, R.D. 3 Canandaigua, N.Y. 14424. A high school teacher, and apprentice to Sun Bear he teaches Earth Awareness, native crafts, and wilderness survival workshops.

Crysalis Mulligan. 1341 Ocean Ave., Apt. 121, Santa Monica, CA 90401. The Bear Tribe Regional Coordinator for Southern California, (213)392-9331.

R. Carlos Nakai. A composer and musician, visual artist and teacher, the music produced by his handcrafted wooden flutes can be described as hauntingly beautiful, timeless, and rejuvenating.

Edith Newcomb (Willow Woman). A teacher of the native American path. For more information on workshops contact: Edith Newcomb, Rt. 2, Box 11, Moyers WV 26813.

Nimimosha. She teaches Earth Awareness workshops and does Medicine Wheel consultations. She can be contacted in care of the Bear Tribe, P.O. Box 9167, Spokane, WA 99209-9167, (509)326-6561.

Gwen and Tom Oaks. Gwen is a student of holistic health and a well known practitioner of crystal consciousness. She holds regular workshops in crystal therapy. She is an apprentice to Sun Bear, and director of the Earth Awareness workshop program for the Bear Tribe. She is also a writer. Tom and Gwen are teachers of beautiful loving workshops that embrace Earth Awareness and wilderness appreciation. Tom and Gwen are the main people to contact for earth awareness workshops in your area. For more information or brochures contact: Gwen and Tom Oaks, 824 Zion St., Nevada City, CA 95959. 916-265-4144

Autumn Parramore. The owner and practitioner of the Color Therapy Clinic Healthworks in Seattle, (206)632-4454.

Saundra Pathweaver. The Bear Tribe Regional Coordinator for Eastern Washington, she teaches Earth Awareness workshops and does Medicine Wheel consultations. She can be contacted in care of the Bear Tribe, P.O. Box 9167, Spokane, WA 99209-9167 (509)326-6561.

Darlene Pearson. 4940 Jean Brilliant, Montreal, Quebec H3W, T7, Canada. The Bear Tribe Regional Coordinator for Canada.

Slow Turtle (John Peters). He is the Director of Indian Affairs for the State of Massachusetts and a medicine man for the Wampanoag Nation.

Lee Piper. The author of traditional native children's stories, a counselor, and teacher, she is the Bird Clan Mother of the Eastern Cherokee Overhill Band.

Dennis Price. 1646 Funston Street North, Hollywood, FL 33020. The Bear Tribe regional coordinator in Florida, Dennis is a fireman/paramedic, massage therapist, and teacher.

Dila Provost. General Delivery, Brocket, Alberta, Canada TOR 040. An alcohol counsellor, and long time apprentice to Sun Bear.

Jan Pohl. P.O. Box 230862, Anchorage, AK 99523. The Bear Tribe Regional Coordinator for Alaska.

Sue Powell and Lou Prisco. Their interest is in assisting their friends of the crystal kingdom on their healing journey of destiny, to the right person or place where they can do the most possible good. Contact them at: Sue Powell and Lou Prisco, 257 Cambon Ave., St. James, NY 11780, (516)862-7518.

Shabari Redbird. She is a ceremonial leader and teacher, and longtime apprentice to Sun Bear. c/o Ananda Ashram, Sapphire Road, Monroe, NY 10950.

Michael Reddy. Lower Hudson Coordinator, The Bear Tribe, 179 Bay St. NY, NY 10464. (212)885-0776.

Dennis Reedy. The Bear Tribe Regional Coordinator for Colorado and Utah. (303)321-1822.

Gary Reiss. 411 Washington, Cottage Grove, OR 97424. A psychotherapist, he is the Bear Tribe Regional Coordinator for Oregon.

Elisabeth Turtle Heart Robinson. Elisabeth Turtle Heart is director of the Earthstone Institute, and coordinator of Vision Quest programs for the Bear Tribe. She also teaches in the Teaching Earth Awareness programs, the Medicine Wheel Consultation programs, and apprentice screenings. She can be contacted at the Bear Tribe, P.O. Box 9167, Spokane, WA 99209-9167. (509)326-6561.

Alma Rose and Gil Milner. Holistic health practitioners and facilitators of workshops, Gil is a psychiatrist and is a western and Chinese medical practitioner. For a brochure or more information contact: Alma Rose and Gil Milner, 16 W. 18th, Spokane, WA 99209. (509)747-6401.

Nate Scarritt. P.O. Box 409, Gardner, KS 66030. A businessman working in the manufacturing and mail ordering of boating accessories, he is an Earth Encounter teacher and the Bear Tribe Regional Coordinator for Kansas, Nebraska, and Oklahoma.

Holly Schuck. 3400 16th Ave. South, Minneapolis, MN 55407. A juvenile corrections officer and the Bear Tribe Regional Coordinator for North and South Dakota, Minnesota, and Wisconsin, Holly also organizes "Indian Summer" canoe trips.

Nicki Scully. A featured speaker at many women's and herbal retreats, she shares her unique teachings of the Egyptian Huna and of the Cauldron Teachings.

Shawnodese. c/o The Bear Tribe, P.O. Box 9167, Spokane, WA 99209. Shawnodese is one of Sun Bear's medicine helpers, the former director of the apprentice program, and an internationally known lecturer and teacher. He has worked with crystals, dreams, and other elements of holistic living since the late 1960s.

Dawn Silver, Healing Earth Resources (H.E.R.), 2570 North Lincoln Avenue, Chicago, IL 60614, 312-EARTH ext. 59. Dawn is a holistic health practitioner who is a graduate of the Chicago National College of Naprapathy. She is also a co-owner of

H.E.R., a store dedicated to carrying products that respect the coming earth changes.

Dawn Songfeather. 14427 N.E. Kelly Rd., Duvall WA 98019. Dawn has studied with Wabun, Sun Bear, and Tom Brown. She teaches about earth spirituality, the feminine, and women's moon time.

Michael G. Smith, P.O. Box 26881, Lakewood, CO 80226. He is a psychic healer and the contemporary discoverer of the crystal power rod, and other crystal devices, that he feels date back to the time of Atlantis. He is the author of *Crystal Power*, published by Llewellyn Publications.

Starhawk. The author of *Dreaming The Dark: Magic, Sex And Politics, The Spiral Dance* and *Truth Or Dare: Encounters With Power, Authority and Mystery.* She is a political activist, writer, counsellor, and ritualist.

Cheryl Starsong. A Medicine Wheel Consultant, she does graphics and database management. Contact her through The Earthstone Institute, P.O. Box 9167, Spokane, WA 99209-9167.

Renate Straub. Bahnhofstrasse 41, 8963 Waltenhofen, West Germany. The Bear Tribe Regional Coordinator for Munich, West Germany.

Luisah Teish. The author of the book *Jambalaya*, she is a priestess of Oshun in the Afro-American tradition of Yoruba/Lacumi. A dancer, storyteller, and spiritual counsellor, Luisah leads workshops and teaches classes throughout the United States on shamanistic practices and religious beliefs.

Red Hawk (Charlie Thom). He is a full-blooded Yurok from northern California who has been practicing the medicine way for over fifty years. Much of his out-reach work is through the Sweatlodge Purification Ceremony which he says is the "fastest way to turn people around."

Barbara Tilmann-Kauf. Bismarkstrasse 16, 8130 Starnberg, West Germany. A naturopath in Germany, and a Bear Tribe networker there.

Ruth (Moon Deer) Traut. An apprentice to Sun Bear, coordinator of native American and earth healing workshops and teacher of Apprentice and Vision Quest programs. For more information or brochures contact: Ruth Traut, The Bear Tribe, P.O. Box 9167, Spokane, WA 99209.

Adam Trombly. A world renowned physicist and the director of Project Earth, he applies his global vision to his work in trying to save the Earth Mother from being consumed by pollution and irresponsible development.

Ken Trogden. 1921 Pickens, Suite B, Columbia, SC 29201. A clinical psychologist, and vision guide.

Pat Tuholuske. A horticulturist, herbalist and creator of "Eartherbs." She raises and sells a variety of herbal goods through Willow Rain Herb Farm.

Venerable Ngakpa Chogayam Ogyen Togden. A tantric yoga shaman of the ancient traditions of Tibet, he belongs to the White lineage of nomadic and Mountain Dwelling Lamas. Chogayam is an author of several books on the tradition.

Edna Falke Von Hartmann. Beselerstrasse 15A, 2000 Hamburg 52, West Germany. The Bear Tribe regional coordinator for Hamburg, Germany, and a teacher and networker.

Renate and David Wendl-Berry. Flt 3 11 Kingscroft Rd, London NW2 3QE, England. The Bear Tribe Regional Coordinators for London, England.

Laura West, 100 Court Square, Suite A, Charlottesville, VA 22901. Laura is a registered nurse with sixteen years experience in working with childbirth, newborn infants, and dying people. She presently has a private practice in which she uses a variety of holistic methods to help people achieve maximum health.

Margie White. 414 Darby Rd., 1st rear, Havertown, PA 19083. The Bear Tribe Regional Coordinator of the Pennsylvania and New Jersey area along with Judith Brigham and Dixie Carlson.

Ann Wolfe. She has been inspiring audiences for over fifteen years as a singer/songwriter and workshop leader. Her music brings messages of personal transformation, unity, and world peace.

Darry Wood. An earth-oriented artisan and a woodsman of the old scout-craft tradition, he teaches earth skills not as survival techniques but rather as keys to a natural way of living.

Yehwehnode, or Twylah Nitsch (She Whose Voice Rides on the Wind). She is a teacher in the Wolf Clan Lodge and speaks on the wisdom, prophecy, and philosophy of the Seneca people. She is also a respected grandmother and clan mother to the people of the planet.

Appendix B:
A Resource Guide to
Healing the Earth

Following is a list of suggestions of some of the people to whom you can write to voice your complaints about the destruction of our planet. Don't forget to refer to the guidelines in chapter 12 when composing your letters.

FEDERAL

The President
The White House
1600 Pennsylvania Ave., NW
Washington, DC 20500
(202)456-1414

A telegram to the White House can be sent through any Western Union office for approximately $4.25.

The Vice President
Executive Office Building
Washington, DC 20501
(202)456-2326

While congress is in session, United States Senators may be contacted at:

The Senate Office Building
Washington, DC 20515
(202)224-3121

For the local address and phone number of the federal representative for your district, please check the front of your area telephone directory under United States Government.

163

Office of Civilian Radioactive
Waste Management
Department of Energy
1000 Independence Ave., SW
Washington, DC 20585

Nuclear Regulatory Commission
Division of Waste Management
Office of Nuclear Material Safety
  and Standards
1717 H Street, NW
Washington, DC 20555

Environmental Action
1346 Connecticut Ave.
Washington, DC 20036
(202)833-1845

Council on Environmental
  Quality
722 Jackson Place, NW
Washington, DC 20006

Environmental Protection
  Agency
FOI Officer
401 M St. SW
Washington, DC 20406

United States Department of the
  Interior
Geologic Survey Public Inquiries
1028 General Services
  Administration Office
19th and F Streets, NW
Washington, DC 20244

United States Department of the
  Interior
Bureau of Land Management
18th and C Streets, NW
Washington, DC 20244

Office of Hazardous Materials
  Regulation
Materials Transportation Bureau
400 7th Street, SW
Washington, DC 20590

United States Environmental
  Protection Agency
Office of Radiation Programs
401 M Street, SW
Washington, DC 20460

United States Environmental
  Protection Agency
Office of Technology
  Assessment
United States Congress
Washington, DC 20510

Environmental Policy Institute
281 D St. SE
Washington, DC 20003

National Low-Level Waste
  Management Program
EG&G, Idaho, Inc.,
P.O. Box 1625
Idaho Falls, ID 83415

National Resource Defense
  Council
1350 New York Ave. NW
Washington, DC 20005

Nuclear Information and
  Resource Service
1346 Connecticut Ave. NW
Washington, DC 20036

Utility Nuclear Waste
  Management Group
1111 19th St., NW
Washington, DC 20036-3691

United States Geological Survey
Water Resources Division
National Water Data Exchange
Reston, VA 22092
860-7444 or 860-6031
(Knowledgeable on geology and
   groundwater nationwide.)

Nuclear Regulatory Commission
1717 H Street, NW
Washington, DC 20555

Energy Department
Conservation and Renewable
   Energy Inquiry and Referral
   Service
(phone only), (800)523-2929 (toll
   free in the continental United
   States).

Energy Department
Conservation and Renewable
   Energy
Washington, DC 20585

Environmental Protection
   Agency
National Pesticide
   Telecommunications Network
(phone only) (800)585-7378 (toll
   free)

United States Environmental
   Protection Agency
Office of Public Affairs
Washington, DC 20460

United States Environmental
   Protection Agency
Public Information Center
820 Quincy St. NW
Washington, DC 20011

Toxic Substances Control Act
   (TSCA)
Assistance Office
(phone only) (800)424-9065 (toll
   free)

STATE

For the local addresses and phone numbers of the members of the
State Legislature, please check the front of your area telephone
directory under your state, e.g., California, State of.

SOME GROUPS THAT PACK A WALLOP AND MAKE A DIFFERENCE

Canadian Coalition on Acid Rain
3421 M St. NW #1637
Washington, DC 20007

California League of
   Conservation Voters
942 Market St. #608
San Francisco, CA 94102
(415) 397-7780

Heal The Bay: An educational
   organization working to clean
   up Santa Monica Bay
For more information call
   Dorothy Green (213)270-4151

Sierra Club
730 Polk St.
San Francisco, CA 94109

Sierra Club Radioactive Waste
  Campaign
78 Elwood St.
Buffalo, NY 14201

Union of Concerned Scientists
1346 Connecticut Ave. NW
Washington, DC 20036

The Society of Prayer for World
  Peace
5-26-27 Nakakokubun
Ichidawa
Chiba
JAPAN 272.
(Promoting World Peace
  Through Prayer.)

L.A. Green Party
Bob Kochler
(213)478-7946

So. CA Alliance for Survival
1031 6th St.
Santa Monica, CA 90403
(213) 388-1824 or (213)399-1000
  (hotline)
(nuclear issues info)

Coalition For Clean Air
309 Santa Monica Blvd. #312
Santa Monica, CA 90401
(213)451-0651

Conservation International
1015 18th Street, NW, Suite
  1000
Washington, DC 20036
(202)429-5660

Environmental Defense Fund
257 Park Avenue South,
New York, NY 10010
(800)RECYCLE

Sierra Club
330 Pennsylvania Ave. SE,
Washington, DC 20003
(202)547-1141

People for the Ethical Treatment
  of Animals (PETA)
P.O. Box 42516
Washington, DC 20015

Sea Shepherd Society
Box 7000-S
Redondo Beach, CA 90277

Environmental Defense Fund
1616 P Street, NW
Washington, DC 20077-6048

Greenpeace
P.O. Box 3720
Washington, DC 20007
Or PO Box 96099
Washington, DC 20090-6099

Amnesty International USA
322 Eighth Ave.,
New York, NY 10117-0389

World Wildlife Fund
1250 24th St., NW
Washington, DC 20037

The Wilderness Society
1400 Eye St., NW
Washington, DC 20005

National Humane Education
  Society
211 Gibson St., NW
104 Jackson Building
Leesburg, VA 22075

Common Cause
P.O. Box 220
Washington, DC 20077-1275

Natural Resources Defense
Council
122 E. 42nd St.
New York, NY 10168

Humane Society of the United
States
2100 L St., NW
Washington, DC 20037

National Abortion Rights Action
League
Box 336
2040 Polk Street
San Francisco, CA 94109

The Nature Conservancy
1815 North Lynn St.
Arlington, VA 22209

National Wildlife Federation,
1400 Sixteenth St., N.W.
Washington, DC 20036-2266

Earth Island Institute
300 Broadway
San Francisco, CA 94133

Cousteau Society
930 West 21st St.
Norfolk, VA 23517

Fund for the Feminist Majority
P.O. Box 96042
Washington, DC 20077

The National Organization for
Women
1401 New York Ave.
Washington, DC 20005

The American Civil Liberties
Union
132 W. 43rd St.
New York, NY 10036

Planned Parenthood Federation
of America
810 Seventh Avenue
New York, NY 10019

Bibliography

Airola, Paavo Ph.D., N.D. *How To Get Well*. Phoenix, Arizona: Health Plus Publishers, 1974.

Alexander, Dale. *Arthritis & Commonsense*. New York: Simon and Shuster, 1981.

Atkins, Robert C., M.D. *Dr. Atkins Nutrition Breakthrough: How to Treat Your Medical Condition Without Drugs*. New York: Bantam, 1981.

Bach, Edward, M.D. and F. J. Wheeler, M.D. *The Bach Flower Remedies*. New Canaan, Connecticut: Keats Publishing, 1979.

Baker, Elizabeth and Dr. Elton Baker. *The Uncook Book*. Saguache, Colorado: Communication Creativity, 1984.

Barnaby, Frank. *The Gaia Peace Atlas*. New York: Doubleday Dell Publishing Group, Inc., 1986.

Bradshaw, John. *The Family*. Pompano Beach, Florida: Health Communications, 1985.

Brown, Tom, Jr. *Tom Brown's Guide to Wild Edible and Medicinal Plants*. New York: The Berkley Publishing Group, 1984.

———. *Tom Brown's Field Guide To Wilderness Survival*. New York: The Berkley Publishing Group, 1984.

Butler, Kurt and Lynn Rayner, M.D. *The Best Medicine: The Complete Health and Preventive Medicine Handbook*. San Francisco: Harper and Row, 1985.

Chivian, Susan, Eric Chivian, M.D., Robert Jay Lifton, M.D., and John E. Mack *Last Aid*. New York: W.H. Freeman and Company, 1982.

Cousins, Norman. *Anatomy of an Illness*. New York: Bantam Books, 1982.

Davidson, Victor S., N.D., D.O. *Iridiagnosis*. Wellingborough, England: Thorsons Publishers Limited, 1979.

Davis, Francyne. *The Low Blood Sugar Cookbook*. New York: Bantam Books, 1982.

Densmore, Frances. *How Indians Use Wild Plants for Food, Medicine and Crafts*. New York: Dover Publications, 1974.

Diamond, Harvey and Marilyn Diamond. *Fit For Life*. New York: Warner Books, 1987.

169

Dolfyn. *Crystal Wisdom: A Beginner's Guide.* Atlanta: Dolfyn, 1984.

Ewald, Ellen Buchman. *Recipes for a Small Planet.* New York: Ballantine Books, 1980.

Gifford, Susan Jean. *Choices and Connections.* Boulder, Colorado: Human Potential Resources, 1987.

Griffith, H. Winter. *Complete Guide to Vitamins, Minerals and Supplements.* Tucson, Arizona: Fisher Books, 1988.

Haas, Elson M, M.D. *Staying Healthy with the Seasons.* Milbrae, California: Celestial Arts, 1981.

Hall, Dorothy. *The Herb Tea Book,* New Canaan, Connecticut: Keats Publishing, 1981.

Hutchens, Alma R. *Indian Herbalogy of North America,* Ontario: Merco, 1983.

Jackins, Harvey. *The Upwards Trend.* Seattle: Rational Island Publishers, 1978.

Kadans, Joseph M. Ph.D. *Encyclopedia of Fruits, Vegetables, Nuts and Seeds for Healthful Living.* West Nyack, New York: Parker Publishing Company, 1973.

Keyes, Ken, Jr. *The Hundredth Monkey.* Coos Bay, Oregon: Vision Books, 1982.

Kloss, Jethro. *Back to Eden,* Loma Linda, California: Back to Eden Books, 1939.

Kubler-Ross, Elisabeth. *On Death and Dying.* New York: Macmillan, 1969.

Kulvinskas, Viktoras, M.S. *Live Food Longevity Recipies.* Fairfield, Iowa: 21st Century Publications, 1984.

Kushner, Harold S. *When Bad Things Happen to Good People.* New York: Avon Books, 1981.

League of Woman Voters Education Fund, The. *The Nuclear Waste Primer.* New York: Nick Lyons Books, 1985.

Logan, Elizabeth A. *Crystal Cosmos Connection: A Network Directory.* Winnipeg, Manitoba: Crystal Cosmos Network, 1988.

Lowen, Alexander, M.D. *Bioenergetics.* New York: Penguin Books Limited, 1975.

Lowen, Alexander, M.D. *Pleasure, A Creative Approach to Life,* New York: Penguin Books, 1970.

Lyon, Lisa and Douglas Kenthall. *Lisa Lyon's Body Magic.* New York: Bantam Books, 1981.

Magnuson, Ed. "They Lied to Us." *Time* 132 (1988) 60–65.

Manning, Russell. *Wheatgrass Juice.* Calastoga, California: Greenward Press, 1979.

Mindell, Earl. *Vitamin Bible.* New York: Warner Books, 1985.

Murphy, Joseph D.R.S., D.D., Ph.D., LL.D. *Within You Is the Power.* Marina Del Rey, California: De Voss and Company, 1977.

Null, Gary and Steven Null. *Poisons in Your Body.* New York: Arco, 1984.

Olinekova, Gayle. *Go for It!* New York: Simon & Shuster, 1982.

Oliver, Martha H. *Add a Few Sprouts, To Eat Better for Less Money.* New Canaan, Connecticut: Keats Publishing, 1975.

Passwater, Richard, Ph.D. *Super Calorie, Carbohydrate Counter.* New York: Dale Books, 1978.

Pearson, Durk and Sandy Shaw. *Life Extension: A Practical Scientific Approach.* New York: Warner Books, 1982.

Peck, M. Scott, M.D. *The Road Less Traveled.* New York: Simon and Shuster, 1984.

Powell, John, S.J. *Why Am I Afraid to Tell You Who I Am?* Allen, Texas: Argus Communications, 1969.

Pritikin, Nathan with Patrick M. McGrady, Jr. *The Pritikin Program for Diet & Exercise.* New York: Gross and Dunlap, 1984.

Randolf, Theron G., M.D. and Ralph W. Moss, M.D. *An Alternative Approach to Allergies.* New York: Bantam Books, 1980.

Rudolph, Theodore M., Ph.D. *Chlorophyll, Nature's "Green Magic."* San Jacinto, California: Nutritional Research, 1982.

Scholl, Lisette. *Visionetics, The Holistic Way to Better Eyesight.* Garden City, New York: Doubleday & Company, 1978.

Sorensen, Jacki. *Aerobic Dancing.* New York: Rawson Wade, 1977.

Sun Bear. *Buffalo Hearts.* Spokane, Washington: Bear Tribe Publishing, 1976.

Sun Bear. *At Home in the Wilderness.* Happy Camp, California: Naturegraph Publishers, 1968.

Sun Bear & Wabun, with Nimimosha. *The Bear Tribe's Self-Reliance Book.* New York: Prentice Hall Press, 1988.

Sun Bear & Wabun. *The Medicine Wheel Earth Astrology.* New York: Prentice Hall Press, 1980.

Sun Bear, Wabun, and Barry Weinstock. *Sun Bear: The Path of Power.* New York: Prentice Hall Press, 1987.

Thie, John F. D.C. *Touch for Health.* Marina del Ray, California: DeVross & Company, 1979.

Tierra, Michael, C.A., N.D. *The Way of Herbs.* New York: Washington Square Press, 1983.

Tomkins, Peter. *Secret Life of Plants.* New York: Harper & Row, 1973.

Whittlesey, Marietta. *Killer Salt.* New York: Avon Books, 1978.

Wind, Wabun and Anderson Reed. *Lightseeds.* New York: Prentice Hall Press, 1988.

Woititz, Janet Geringer, Ed.D. *Adult Children of Alcoholics.* Deerfield Beach, Florida: Health Communications, 1982.

About the Authors

Sun Bear is a Chippewa medicine man who founded The Bear Tribe, located near Spokane, Washington, which welcomes Indians and non-Indians as members. The publisher of the magazine *Wildfire,* he is also a lecturer, teacher, and author of the books *Sun Bear: The Path of Power, At Home in the Wilderness, The Medicine Wheel, Buffalo Hearts,* and *The Bear Tribe's Self-Reliance Book.*

Wabun, his medicine helper, holds an M.S. from Columbia School of Journalism and has written articles for such magazines as *Life, McCall's,* and *New York.* She is the author of the books *The People's Lawyers, Woman of the Dawn,* and *Lightseeds* (with Anderson Reed) and has worked with Sun Bear as coauthor or editor on a variety of his books and publications. She is the founder of *Wind Communications,* a literary agency. She is also a transpersonal practitioner and ceremonial designer.

If you would like to write to Sun Bear or Wabun, their address is:

> Sun Bear and Wabun
> c/o The Bear Tribe
> P.O. Box 9167
> Spokane, WA 99209

Crysalis Mulligan and **Peter (Sentinel Bear) Nufer** teach a variety of survival, earth medicine, and crystal/gemstone mining workshops in addition to founding *Red Road Trading Company* and the *Earth Medicine Newsletter.* Peter (Sentinel Bear) is involved in the film industry and they both participate in many environmental and conservational projects. If you would like to write either of them, or to receive a catalogue, schedule of events, or newsletter, please contact:

> Crysalis or Sentinel Bear
> Red Road Trading Co.
> 1341 Ocean Ave. #121
> Santa Monica, CA 90401